CURRENT ISSUES BIBLE STUDY SERIES

Faith and Work

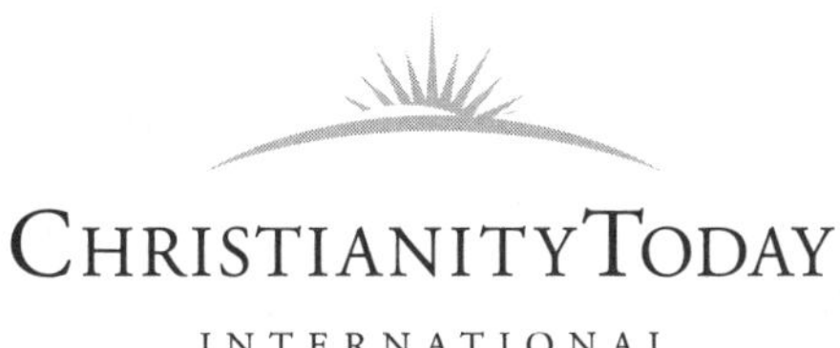

THOMAS NELSON
Since 1798

NASHVILLE DALLAS MEXICO CITY RIO DE JANEIRO BEIJING

OTHER BOOKS IN THIS SERIES

Engaging the Culture
Islam
Politics

Current Issues Bible Study Series: Faith and Work

Published in Nashville, Tennessee, by Thomas Nelson. Thomas Nelson is a registered trademark of Thomas Nelson, Inc.

Thomas Nelson, Inc. titles may be purchased in bulk for educational, business, fundraising, or sales promotional use. For information, please e-mail SpecialMarkets@thomasnelson.com.

Editor: Kelli B. Trujillo
Development Editors: Kelli B. Trujillo and Roxanne Wieman
Associate Editor: JoHannah Reardon
Page Designer: Robin Crosslin

ISBN 13: 978-1-4185-3425-7

Printed in the United States of America
08 09 10 11 12 RRD 6 5 4 3 2 1

CONTENTS

CONTRIBUTING WRITERS

Lynne M. Baab is the author of *Sabbath Keeping: Finding Freedom in the Rhythms of Rest* (InterVarsity). She lives in Washington.

Sarah Franklin Crose works in Human Resources at Christianity Today International and is involved with the Christian ministries of *Life Embraced* and *Camps Farthest Out*.

Jeron Frame is a contributing author to the website ChristianBibleStudies.com, a service of Cristianity Today International.

Randy Frazee is a Teaching Pastor at Willow Creek Community Church and is the author of many books, including *Making Room for Life*.

Christine J. Gardner recently finished her PhD at Northwestern University and is now an assistant professor in the communications department at Wheaton College.

Gary A. Gilles is adjunct instructor at Trinity International University, editor of *Chicago Caregiver* magazine, and a freelance writer.

Steve Jolley is Teaching Pastor at Santa Barbara Community Church in California.

Ginger Kolbaba is an author and the editor of *Marriage Partnership* magazine, a sister publication of *Christianity Today*.

Joy-Elizabeth Lawrence is a freelance writer living in Grand Rapids, Michigan, with her husband.

Penny Schlaf Musco lives and works in New Jersey.

Anne Peterson is a poet, speaker, and regular contributor to ChristianBibleStudies.com.

JoHannah Reardon is associate editor of ChristianBibleStudies.com.

Leland Ryken is Clyde S. Kilby Professor of English at Wheaton College in Wheaton, Illinois.

Bruce Shelley is the senior professor of church history and historical theology at Denver Seminary.

John Throop is president of The Summit Planning Group, a consulting and training firm based in Peoria, Illinois. He also is on the staff of LaSalle County Episcopal Ministry, a four-church parish based in Streator, Illinois. He is the author of two books, *Shape Up from the Inside Out* (Tyndale House Publishers) and *Dealing with Suicide* (David C. Cook).

Kelli B. Trujillo is a writer, editor, and adult ministry leader at her church.

Ramona Cramer Tucker, a regular contributor to *Today's Christian Woman*, is Senior Editor for Tyndale House Publishers. She and her family live in the Chicago area.

INTRODUCTION

We spend nearly half of our waking hours "at work," yet surprisingly for many of us the relationship between our daily work and our faith is a topic often left woefully unaddressed by the church. Is work to be solely a means to an end—an avenue for providing an income? Is work meant to be our mission field—our opportunity to meet and share Christ with non-Christian co-workers? Or are we to find meaning and fulfillment in the work itself?

It's a complex issue that raises all sorts of questions, especially if we don't particularly like our job or if we're working in an environment that brings out the worst in us rather than the best. Whether work for you feels like the daily grind or you've found yourself in your dream job, the discussions in this *Current Issues Bible Study* will help you explore together the significance of work in your life as a Christian—and will challenge you in ways you may not expect.

For Small Groups

These studies are designed to be used in small groups—communities of people with a commitment to and connection with each other. Whether you're an existing small group or you're just planning to meet for the next eight weeks, this resource will help you deepen in your personal faith and grow closer with each other.

Along with the eight studies, you'll find a bonus Small-Group Builder article from *Christianity Today*'s SmallGroups.com. On this website, you'll find everything you need to successfully run a small-groups ministry. The insightful free articles and theme-specific downloads provide expert training. The reproducible curriculum courses bring thought leaders from across the world into your group's discussion at a fraction of the price. And the revolutionary Small Groups Connect social network will help keep your group organized and connected 24/7.

Christianity Today Articles

Each study session begins with one or two thought-provoking articles from *Christianity Today* or one of its sister publications. These articles are meant to help you dive deeply into the topic and engage with a variety of thoughts and opinions. Be sure to read the articles before you arrive to your small group meeting; the time you invest on the front end will greatly enrich your group's discussion. As you read, you may find the articles persuasive and agree heartily with their conclusions; other times you may disagree with the claims of an article, but that's great too. We want these articles to serve as a springboard for lively discussion, so differences in opinion are welcome.

For more insightful articles from *Christianity Today* visit http://www.ctlibrary.com/ and subscribe now.

Timing

These studies are designed to be flexible, with plenty of discussion, activities, and prayer time to fill a full small group meeting. If you'd like, you can zero in on a few questions or teaching points and discuss them in greater depth, or you can aim to spend a few minutes on each question of a given session. Be sure to manage your time so that you're able to spend time on the "Going Forward" questions and prayer time at the end of each study.

Ground Rules

True spiritual growth happens in the context of a vibrant, Christian community. To establish that type of community in your small group, we recommend a few *ground rules*.

- Guarantee confidentiality. Promise together that whatever is said in the context of your small group meeting is kept in that small group meeting. This sense of trust and safety will enable you to more honestly share about your spiritual struggles.
- Participate—with balance. We all have different personalities. Some of us like to talk . . . a lot. Others of us prefer to be quiet. But for this

study to truly benefit your group, everyone needs to participate. Make it a personal goal to answer (aloud) at least half of the discussion questions in a given session. This will allow space for others to talk (lest you dominate discussion too much) but will also guarantee your own contribution is made to the discussion (from which other group members will benefit).

- Be an attentive listener—to each other and to God. As you read Scripture and discuss these important cultural issues, focus with care and love on the other members of your group. These questions are designed to be open-ended and to allow for a diversity of opinion. Be gracious toward others who express views that are different than your own. And even more important, prayerfully remain attentive to the presence of God speaking to and guiding your group through the Holy Spirit.

It is our prayer that this *Current Issues Bible Study* will change the lives of your group members as you seek to integrate your faith into the cultural issues you face everyday. May the Holy Spirit work in and through your group as you challenge and encourage each other in spiritual growth.

Is our work meant to be

a blessing, a curse, or

something else altogether?

Genesis 1:27–31, 2:15, 3:17–19

Ecclesiastes 2:4–11

Colossians 3:22–24

SESSION 1

WORK—DRUDGERY OR DELIGHT?

■

For some people, work is a source of great personal satisfaction—perhaps they're in their "dream job" or maybe they feel they're making a difference in the world. For others, work is a means to an end: the paycheck. For them, work is the daily grind and *TGIF!* is their mantra. Real life starts not when work begins but when it ends.

So is work a blessing or a curse? As followers of Christ, how should we feel about our work, and what should characterize the work we do? Is there an inherent value to work (besides economic necessity)? While most of us will spend a significant portion of our lives on the job, it seems only a few of us find meaning and fulfillment in what we do. Is the secret a new job, or a new attitude toward the one we have? We'll explore these questions and many others using Bruce Shelley's *Christianity Today* article "Why Work?"

■ Before You Meet

Read "Why Work?" by Bruce Shelley from *Christianity Today* magazine.

WHY WORK?

by Bruce Shelley

National news wires reported the death of a self-educated janitor named Lawrence Hummel, who wore his lawyer's hand-me-downs but left over $600,000 to Bethany College in northern West Virginia, where he mopped floors for thirty years.

Hummel had amassed a million-dollar fortune from the stock market with knowledge gleaned from discussions with professors and from economics classes at the college. Even so, to the end of his life Hummel continued to live frugally.

"If you saw him and talked with him," said Joseph Gompers, his lawyer, "you might confuse him with a bum. But he wasn't. He was a warm, compassionate person who cared about people."

—*The Denver Post*, April 20, 1988

The story made news because Lawrence Hummel was different; according to the standards of contemporary American culture, he was even something of a misfit. He saw no need to turn his wealth into any of the normally accepted symbols of the American dream: clothes, travel, homes, or cars. Work, for Hummel, had a higher purpose. Thoughtful Christians have always claimed the same thing—that work has a purpose beyond paychecks and perks.

Restless in the Workplace

Contemporary American culture would give several reasons for work. Perhaps the prevailing one is traceable to Adam Smith's classic treatise, *The Wealth of Nations.* In 1776 the Scottish professor of moral philosophy argued that people work because it is in their enlightened self-interest. "Every individual," Smith wrote, "is continually exerting himself to find out the most advantageous employment for whatever capital he can command." Capitalism, based on Adam Smith's views, then, harnesses our innate selfishness for the "common good."

While capitalism in America has changed dramatically in the last few generations, evidence of the creativity and productivity that it has fostered abounds. We are surrounded by the promises and rewards of the American dream: appliances, cars, conveniences, and toys of all shapes and sizes.

At the same time, thoughtful observers of the American scene have become acutely aware of the dark side of all this: widespread addiction to self-interest, the passion for consumer products, and the empty spirit of today's worker. Many Americans pursuing the economic dream of hot tubs, condos, and money market accounts are apparently growing restless in the workplace.

A poll conducted for Robert Half International, a New York-based accounting firm, indicated that one out of four Americans is unhappy in his or her job. The reasons? Workers most often mentioned their need for greater recognition, more money, less stress, and a better boss.

This frustration in the workplace comes in large part because people feel the squeeze of two conflicting attitudes toward work.

On the one hand, Americans are influenced by the images from our economic culture that portray the workplace as a source of happiness and personal fulfillment. Even when we are not sure how to define work, we know that it is linked somehow with a sense of self. What we *do* is supposed to describe what we *are.*

When an American meets someone for the first time, within minutes the question is asked, "What do you do?" The frequency of the question points to our idolization of jobs in America. We even assess a person's worth according to his or her employment.

Studs Terkel wrote a hefty volume titled *Working* in which he let scores of workers describe their feelings about their jobs. It was obvious that most of them nurtured the dream that they would somehow "find themselves" in their work; and when they suddenly found themselves on the list of the unemployed, they were devastated.

Terkel quoted John R. Coleman, president of Haverford College, who probably expressed the trauma of unemployment best. He had taken an unusual sabbatical, during which he worked at menial jobs. While working as a porter-dishwasher, he was fired.

"I'd never been fired," he recalled, "and I'd never been unemployed. For three days I walked the streets. Though I had a bank account, though my children's tuition was paid, though I had a salary and a job waiting for me back in Haverford, I was demoralized."

On the other hand, recent years have convinced many Americans that work can never be satisfying in itself. Many of us endure work only so long as it promises a satisfactory private life. Work, more recent American culture would have us believe, is simply a necessary evil of physical existence, a mere means to personal pleasure.

Americans subscribing to this line of thinking live from one coffee break to another. When it comes to weekends, "TGIF," they say: "Thank God, it's Friday!" Work is the place to accumulate the cash for another escape to Maui or the Bahamas. So a job for these Americans is always a barrier to happiness, never a way of happiness.

Can't we catch the same attitude in our television commercials? One of them showed four friends in their fishing clothes, surrounded by a breathtaking mountain scene. They were sitting around a warm, glowing fire. The fish were in the skillet and the beer was on ice. With everyone smiling, one of the men held up a chilled can and said, "It just doesn't get any better than this."

The point is obvious: Life isn't found on the job accomplishing something significant. It is found instead with friends, outdoors, on a weekend, with food and a special beer.

The frustration behind this understanding of work has led hosts of Americans today to abandon the traditional Puritan work ethic. According to sociologist Daniel Bell, their capitalism survives but without the advantage of any moral or transcendent ethic. They work with no overarching purpose. In *The Cultural Contradictions,* he claims this creates "an extraordinary contradiction within the social structure itself." For on the one hand, he writes, "the business corporation wants an individual to work hard, pursue a career, accept delayed gratification—to be, in the crude sense, an organization man. And yet, in its products and its advertisements, the corporation promotes pleasure, instant joy, relaxing, and letting go."

Work in the Bible

What is the Christian alternative to the raw self-interest of the American dream? The Bible teaches that work is ordained of God, for our benefit.

That is the significance of the Christian view of work. In their book *Why Work?*, John Bernbaum and Simon Steer summarize the biblical teaching with five basic principles:

First, *work is God-ordained.* According to the Genesis story of Creation, the command to work comes from One who is himself a worker. Work was not a result of sinful rebellion; it was a part of God's original intention for human beings. According to Genesis, God commands humanity to "fill the earth and subdue it. Rule over the fish of the sea and the birds of the air and over every living creature" (Gen. 1:28, NIV). We work, then, because God intended us to work.

Second, *as a result of fundamental human rebellion against God, work no longer brings the fulfillment and joy God intended.* Human rebellion is reflected in human work. Work can now become a means of exploitation and oppression, or it can become an idol.

The teacher of Ecclesiastes is a striking example of our human frustration. "I built houses for myself," he writes, "and planted vineyards. . . . I bought male and female slaves. . . . I amassed silver and gold for myself. . . . Yet when I surveyed all that my hands had done . . . everything was meaningless, a chasing after the wind" (Eccles. 2:4–11, NIV).

Third, *Jesus Christ has redeemed our work from the curse.* That the incarnate God worked at a carpenter's bench is a striking testimony to the sanctity of the workplace.

Fourth, *for the Christian, work is to be done as a service to Christ.* "Slaves," wrote the apostle Paul, "whatever you do, work at it with all your heart, as working for the Lord, not for men, since you know that you will receive an inheritance from the Lord as a reward. It is the Lord Christ you are serving" (Col. 3:22–24, NIV).

Finally, *the Bible tells us that work not only brings glory to God if done for him, but has moral benefits as well.* In 2 Thessalonians 3:10–12,

Paul tells us that we should work to provide for ourselves and our families. And in Ephesians 4:28 he urges believers to undertake work that is useful, that we may have "something to share with those in need."

A Christian's View

In our time it is almost impossible for Americans to see how their work can be useful and serve the community at large. The growth of cities and the organization of labor have "privatized" work. Americans have come to look upon their work almost exclusively in terms of personal advantages. Any benefit for the community—beyond economic growth—has largely dropped from view.

Christians, however, are governed by a higher conception of work. In the collect for Labor Day, the Episcopal *Book of Common Prayer* entreats God, "So guide us in the work we do, that we may do it not for self alone, but for the common good." This concern for the "common good" can make work more than a private enterprise.

"The entrepreneur who creates hundreds of new jobs," writes Denver's Catholic Archbishop J. Francis Stafford in *This Home of Freedom,* "is performing a morally good act: he or she is giving fellow human beings an opportunity to exercise their capacity for honest work. Workers who perform their duties conscientiously and well, and trade unions which bargain in good faith for the rights of workers, are also moral agents, contributing to the integrity of the workplace."

We should remember that the colonial Puritans who shaped so much of our thinking about work spoke of work as *vocation.* The word carries the thought that our work is a calling from God. The Lord himself, it implies, has a purpose for every person's work, whether as a nurse, a pilot, a social worker, a lawyer, a mechanic, or, as Jesus, a carpenter.

Certain vocations, it is true, more directly influence the thinking and viewpoints of people in society. Teachers, scriptwriters, politicians, editors, judges, artists, and ministers all fall into this category; they address questions of life and its meaning. Because Christians hold a special view about the kind of creatures we are and what is in store for us in the future, Christians in these "meaning of life" vocations carry a special responsibility to communicate the Christian view of the world. And when they do, they will make a difference in American life.

In many other vocations the questions of ultimate purpose and human destiny never affect the quality of the work itself. A plumber's work itself, for example, never addresses the question of life's meaning. But in these sorts of vocations, the Christian reflects his or her faith in another way, through the care given to the work itself. A Christian plumber therefore works honestly and does the best work he can.

Quality Is Job One

Whether we directly influence others in our jobs or reflect our faith more indirectly through our handiwork, Jesus's workbench suggests to us something about the importance of the quality of our daily work. Who, after all, can imagine Jesus turning out shoddy work? The biblical term for *carpenter* suggests a craftsman. In the earlier days, and still today in many places, in small towns like Nazareth, there were village craftsmen, handymen who could repair a gate, build useful cabinets, or make a set of table and chairs.

That is the kind of work Jesus did. The drawers of the cabinets ran smoothly, the yokes were well balanced, the boxes were square, and the toys were sturdy and safe.

Why does that sound like "the good old days"? Has quality slipped from the American workplace?

Addison H. Leitch, the late Presbyterian professor at Gordon-Conwell Theological Seminary, wrote not long before he died about how he once made himself unpopular at a college convocation at the end of a semester when everyone was getting ready to go home for the holidays.

"Suppose," Leitch said, "that the last man to check out the jet plane on which you will fly home did his job just as faithfully as you have done yours here during the last semester."

A groan went up. The students all knew that the man on the jet can be depended on to do the *right* thing.

But *did* they know that? In a day of dirty restaurants, trains that crash, television repairmen who don't "fix it," police who take bribes, and students who lift books from libraries, how did they know that the maintenance man would do his job?

Quality is a Christian concern because for the Christian the daily job is a daily offering to God. It is never a mere matter of personal choice.

That perspective is vital today. Americans are trying to conduct business, run companies, and get ahead with little concern for standards of right and wrong. Morality, we like to think, is a personal matter. "The business of America is business," some say.

But Christians know better. Like Lawrence Hummel, they have an unusual view of work. They hold that the gospel brings responsibility, dignity, and purpose to what happens in the shop or office. Jesus Christ, their Savior and Model, was, after all, a carpenter. And God has purposes for our work that go far beyond our day-to-day tasks.

Bruce Shelley is the senior professor of church history and historical theology at Denver Seminary. ("Why Work?" was originally published in Christianity Today, *July 14, 1989.)*

■ Open Up

Select one of these activities to launch your discussion time.

Option 1

Discuss one of these icebreaker questions:

- What's the first image that comes to mind when you think of the word *work*?

- What feelings does the word *work* evoke in you? Why?

- What do you think are the common attitudes or mind-sets people have about work in our world? Brainstorm several together as a group.

Option 2

Identify two opposite walls in your meeting room as Wall #1 and Wall #2, then stand together in the middle of the room. Read each of the following questions together as a group; after each question, every person should walk to a spot in the room to show his or her answer.

- What's your general reaction to the word *work*? Treat the room as a scale, stretching from "very negative" (Wall #1) to "very positive" (Wall #2). Walk to a spot in the room that best represents your answer.

- How much happiness or fulfillment do you find in your own job or daily work? Treat the room as a scale, stretching from "zero happiness or fulfillment" (Wall #1) to "a great deal of happiness and fulfillment" (Wall #2). Go to a spot in the room that indicates your answer.

- Using the same scale, how much happiness or fulfillment do you experience in your time away from your job or daily work (during time off)?

- Consider these two viewpoints and determine which one best reflects your perspective? Go to a spot in the room that reflects your answer.

(Wall #1) A person's work should be a source of happiness, meaning, and personal fulfillment.

(Wall #2) Work is a necessary part of existence in order to provide the means to live; but happiness, meaning, and fulfillment usually come outside of one's work.

Return to your seats and take a moment to share your thoughts from this experience.

■ The Issue

Bruce Shelley in his article "Why Work?" says that Americans have lost their sense of the value of work and instead focus on what happens after the work hours. He writes, "This frustration in the workplace comes in large part because people feel the squeeze of two conflicting attitudes toward work.

"On the one hand, Americans are influenced by the images from our economic culture that portray the workplace as a source of happiness and personal fulfillment . . . On the other hand, recent years have convinced many Americans that work can never be satisfying in itself. Many of us endure work only so long as it promises a satisfactory private life."

- How would you answer the question: Why do you work?

- In what ways should work for a Christian be different than it is for someone who has no conscious commitment to God?

■ Reflect

Take a moment to read Genesis 1:27–31, 2:15, 3:17–19; Ecclesiastes 2:4–11; and Colossians 3:22–24. Jot down a few notes and observations about the passages: What do these passages say about work? Which words or phrases stand out to you the most? What questions or issues do these passages raise for you?

■ Let's Explore

Work was part of God's good creation.

- Describe what you do in a typical day at your "job." (For some, this may be a job you do without financial compensation.)

- In your description, did you tend to talk about your work in generally negative or positive terms? What did you focus on . . . and why?

Though work was included in the curse after the Fall (in Genesis 3:17–19), work was not created as a punishment. In fact, God modeled work and rest for the first seven days of creation and he gave humankind work to do from the beginning days in the Garden of Eden.

- Read Genesis 1:27–31, 2:15. What work did God give the first humans? In what tone is the work described? What insights does this give you about God's intention for humans and work?

- In what ways can work be "very good"? Describe a time in your life when you experienced work as a "very good" thing.

- Think of your current work, whether it's a job you are paid for or work you do without financial compensation. What are the best aspects of your job—the tasks or moments that bring you joy or satisfaction?

Because of sin, our experience of work can be far from "very good."

- Do you think some types of jobs more easily lend themselves to being a "delight"—a source of purpose or enjoyment—than others? If so, give examples of jobs that are fulfilling and jobs that seem to be inherently less fulfilling. If not, explain why not.

Read Ecclesiastes 2:4–11.

- Can you relate to the author of Ecclesiastes? When have you felt like this?

Read Genesis 3:17–19. Here, as a consequence of Adam and Eve's sin, Adam's work farming (which was originally "very good") is now described by God in terms of pain and toil.

- When has your job felt like toil or caused pain in your life? What are some of the most difficult or frustrating aspects of your current job?

As followers of Jesus, our work can serve a higher purpose.

In his article, Shelley says that "Christians . . . are governed by a higher conception of work. In the collect for Labor Day, the Episcopal *Book of Common Prayer* entreats God, 'So guide us in the work we do, that we may do it not for self alone, but for the common good.' This concern for the 'common good' can make work more than a private enterprise."

- Reconsider some of the jobs you discussed earlier which seem inherently less fulfilling. In what ways could these jobs be performed by Christians as ways of contributing to the common good?

When it comes to awful jobs, being a slave is the worst of the worst. Yet Paul asserts that even work done in such a demeaning role can have great meaning and can serve a higher purpose. Read Colossians 3:22–24.

- What would it look like for you to do your job as if you are working for Jesus? How would it change your daily work experience? Be specific.

Jesus himself worked as a carpenter (see Mark 6:3). Shelley cites the article *Why Work?* and summarizes one of the author's points this way: "That the incarnate God worked at a carpenter's bench is a striking testimony to the sanctity of the workplace."

- Take a moment to imagine Jesus at work as a craftsman. Why does it matter to you that Jesus himself had a job? How does considering Jesus at work affect your understanding of the place of work in your own life?

■ Going Forward

Break into pairs and discuss these questions.

In his article, Shelley recounts the story of Addison H. Leitch who posed this striking challenge to his seminary students as they prepared to head home at the end of a semester: "Suppose that the last man to check out the jet plane on which you will fly home did his job just as faithfully as you have done yours here during the last semester."

- What if an airline technician or your car mechanic or the construction workers who built the bridge you'll drive across tonight did their jobs "just as faithfully as you have done yours" in recent weeks or months?

- Shelley asserts that "Quality is a Christian concern because for the Christian the daily job is a daily offering to God." Is this statement reflected in your own attitude toward your daily work? Share a specific way in which you feel personally challenged to treat your work as a "daily offering to God."

- What practical steps can you take to recapture God's design and purpose in your job?

Gather back together as a group to pray together. Begin by naming the "delightful" aspects of your various jobs, thanking God for the goodness in the work you do. Then move to a time of prayerful reflection or confession about the parts of your work that feel like "drudgery." Together, ask God to help you do your work unto him and as meaningful service to others.

Want to Explore More?

Recommended Resources

Want to explore this topic further? Here are some resources that will help.

Books

"Why Work?" in *Creed or Chaos?*, Dorothy L. Sayers (Sophia Institute Press; ISBN 091847731X)

Online Resources

"Work *Is* Our Mission," Uwe Siemon-Netto, www.christianitytoday.com/ct/2007/November/30.30.html

"Reflections: Work and Vocation," www.christianitytoday.com/ct/2003/September/19.65.html

"Working to Serve or Serving the Work?" Kelli Trujillo, http://blog.christianitytoday.com/giftedforleadership/2007/09/working_to_serve_or_serving_th.html

www.faithintheworkplace.com

What can we learn

from the Puritans

about work and

vocation?

Exodus 35:30–36:1

Colossians 3:1–17

CALLED . . . TO THIS?!

"The Puritan work ethic" or "the Protestant work ethic" are phrases thrown around these days—usually to describe a person who works lots of overtime, has a high level of responsibility, is efficient, and keeps an unusually spotless desk. But what *is* the Puritan work ethic? Does it really mean an overcommitted and highly efficient employee, or is it something entirely different?

In Leland Ryken's *Christian History & Biography* article "The Original Puritan Work Ethic," we'll learn about three "vintage Puritan traits" regarding attitudes toward work and discuss how we can take these ideas and apply them to the contemporary workplace.

■ Before You Meet

Read "The Original Puritan Work Ethic" by Leland Ryken from *Christian History & Biography* magazine.

THE ORIGINAL PURITAN WORK ETHIC

By valuing all of life in relation to God, Puritans gave sacred significance to every activity.

by Leland Ryken

Suffering from poor health all his life, Richard Baxter preached, he said, "as never sure to preach again, and as a dying man to dying men." Living daily in the shadow of eternity gave the Puritans a deep appreciation for living every moment on this earth to the fullest for God. "Promise not long life to yourselves," Baxter advised, "but live as those that are always uncertain of another day."

For the Puritans, to "redeem the time" (as Baxter put it) meant to order one's daily life in accordance with godly principles and for maximum effectiveness. One of the Puritans' favorite epithets was *well-ordered.* Their opponents nicknamed them the *disciplinarians*. The Puritans aspired to be worldly saints—Christians with earth as their sphere of activity and with heaven as their ultimate hope. Baxter exhorted his readers, "Write upon the doors of thy shop and chamber . . . This is the time on which my endless life dependeth."

This approach to life resulted in three vintage Puritan traits: the ideal of the God-centered life, the doctrine of calling or vocation, and the conviction that all of life is God's.

The God-centered Life

The Puritans' sense of priorities in life was one of their greatest strengths. Putting God first and valuing everything else in relation to God was a recurrent Puritan theme.

Baxter's parting advice to his parishioners at Kidderminster was to "be sure to maintain a constant delight in God." Preaching before the Houses of Parliament, Cornelius Burges admonished everyone present "to lift up his soul to take hold of God, to be glued and united to him . . . to be only his forever."

For the Puritans, the God-centered life meant making the quest for spiritual and moral holiness the great business of life. "In a divine commonwealth," wrote Baxter, "holiness must have the principal honor and encouragement, and a great difference be made between the precious and the vile." Our own culture has conspired to make such holiness seem burdensome, but the Puritans found it an appealing prospect. Ralph Venning, in a book-length treatise on sin, called holiness "the beauty of earth and Heaven, without which we cannot live well on earth, nor shall ever live in Heaven."

Of course, it takes vigilance over one's actions to produce a holy lifestyle. Very tellingly, the Puritans repeatedly used such words as *watching, exact walking*, and *mortification* to describe their preferred lifestyle.

In Puritan thinking, the Christian life was a heroic venture, requiring a full quota of energy. "Christianity is not a sedentary profession or employment," wrote Baxter, adding, "Sitting still will lose you heaven, as well as if you run from it." The Puritans were the activists of their day. In a letter to the Speaker of the House of Commons, Oliver Cromwell crossed out the words *wait on* and made his statement read "who *have wrestled with* God for a blessing."

Stressing the God-centered life can lead to an otherworldly withdrawal from everyday earthly life. For the Puritans, it produced the opposite. Richard Sibbes sounded the keynote: "The life of a Christian is wondrously ruled in this world, by the consideration and meditation of the life of another world." The doctrinal matrix that equipped the Puritans to integrate the two worlds was their thoroughly developed ideas on calling or vocation.

The Puritan Doctrine of Vocation

The Puritans spoke of two callings—a general calling and a particular calling. The general calling is the same for everyone and consists of a call to conversion and godliness. "The general calling," wrote William Perkins, "is the calling of Christianity, which is common to all that live in the church of God. . . . [It] is that whereby a man is called out of the world to be a child of God."

A particular calling consists of the specific tasks and occupations that God places before a person in the course of daily living. It focuses on, but is not limited to, the work that a person does for a livelihood. Several important corollaries follow from this doctrine of vocation.

Since God is the one who calls people to their work, the worker becomes a steward who serves God. Thomas Manton thus commented that "every creature is God's servant, and hath his work to do wherein to glorify God; some in one calling, some in another."

Secondly, the Puritan view that God calls all workers to their tasks in the world dignifies all legitimate kinds of work. Above all, the Puritan doctrine of vocation sanctifies common work. William Tyndale said that if we look externally "there is difference betwixt washing of dishes, and preaching of the word of God; but as touching to please God, none at all." Baxter explained how this could be: "God looketh not . . . principally at the external part of the work, but much more to the heart of him that doth it."

The Puritan doctrine of vocation (inherited, we should note, from Luther and later Continental Reformers) integrated life in the world with the spiritual life. The spiritual life was no longer limited to some "sacred" space, nor was it reserved for monks and nuns who had retired from the world. Instead, it is "in your shops" (said Richard Steele in his classic treatise *The Tradesman's Calling*) "where you may most confidently expect the presence and blessing of God."

This view of work as vocation offers more than simply the possibility of serving God in one's daily work. It offers the possibility of serving God through or by means of that work. To work is to serve God. Baxter's exhortation was for workers to "serve the Lord in serving their masters."

There is a moral dimension to work as well. When the Puritans spoke of the rewards of work, they almost automatically paired serving God with serving humanity. "The main end of our lives," wrote Perkins, "is to serve God in the serving of men in the works of our callings."

If daily work is as central to the spiritual life as the Puritan doctrine of vocation asserts, it is no wonder that the Puritans threw themselves with such zest into their work. We need, of course, to draw a distinction between the original Puritan work ethic and the secularized perversion that followed. The original Puritan work ethic was this: "Be laborious and diligent in your callings . . . and if you cheerfully serve [God] in the labour of your hands, with a heavenly and obedient mind, it will be as acceptable to him as if you had spent all that time in more spiritual exercises" (Baxter).

All of Life is God's

An additional genius of the Puritans was the skill with which they managed to view all of life as God's. The Puritans lived simultaneously in two worlds. For them, both worlds were equally real, and life was not divided into sacred and secular.

According to Thomas Gouge, Christians should "so spiritualize our hearts and affections that we may have heavenly hearts in earthly employments." "If God be God over us," wrote Peter Bulkeley, "he must be over us in every thing."

It is no wonder, then, that the Puritans saw God in the commonplace. Richard Baxter asked his readers, "Canst not thou think on the several places thou hast lived in and remember that they have each had their several mercies?" John Bunyan asked in the preface to *Grace Abounding*, "Have you forgot . . . the milkhouse, the stable, the barn, and the like, where God did visit your soul?"

In such a framework, there are no "trivial" events, and all of life is potentially a teachable moment. One Sunday morning when the young Robert Blair had stayed home from church he looked out of the window to see "the sun brightly shining, and a cow with a full udder," Blair remembered that the sun was made to give light and the cow to give milk, which made him realize how little he understood the purpose of his own life. Shortly thereafter, he was converted while listening to a sermon.

There was no place where the Puritans did not find God. They were always open to what Baxter called "a drop of glory" that God might allow to fall upon their souls.

C. S. Lewis wrote enthusiastically of "the beautiful, cheerful integration of [William] Tyndale's world. He utterly denies the medieval distinction between religion and secular life." Such integration is one of the most attractive features of the Puritans. Their goal was an ordered and disciplined daily life that integrated personal piety, corporate life, everyday work, and the worship of God.

Leland Ryken is Clyde S. Kilby Professor of English at Wheaton College in Wheaton, Illinois. ("The Original Puritan Work Ethic" was first published in Christian History & Biography *on January 1, 2006.)*

Open Up

Select one of these activities to launch your discussion time.

Option 1

Discuss one of these icebreaker questions:

DO'S AND DON'TS IN THE WORKPLACE

From Richard Baxter's *A Christian Directory* (1673)

- Choose that employment or calling . . . in which you may be most serviceable to God. Choose not that in which you may be most rich or honourable in the world.
- Be diligent in your callings, and spend no time in idleness, and perform your labours with holy minds, to the glory of God, and in obedience to his commands.
- Idleness is robbing God, who is the Lord of us and all our faculties.
- Take pleasure in your work, and then you will not be slothful in it.
- This interest of God in your lowest, and hardest, and servilist labour, doth make it honourable and should make it sweet.

- People often use the phrase "work ethic," such as saying "He has a really good work ethic." What is a good work ethic, in your opinion?

- Share an example of someone you know who has a good work ethic. Or, alternately, describe the behavior of someone you've observed to have a poor work ethic.

- The question is, How they use that which they labour so hard for, and save so sparingly. If they use it for God, and charitable uses, there is no man taketh a righter course.
- Remember that riches do make it much harder for a man to be saved.
- If God show you a way in which you may lawfully get more than in another way (without wrong to your soul, or to any other), if you refuse this, and then choose the less gainful way, you cross one of the ends of your calling, and you refuse to be God's steward.
- You must not desire nor seek to get another's goods or labour for less than it is worth.
- You have far more cause to be afraid of prosperity, than of adversity; of riches, than of poverty.
- The devil suiteth his temptations to men's daily work and business.

Option 2

Most people have had quite a few different jobs in their lifetime. Write down (if you can remember!) all the jobs you've ever had. When you're finished, rank the jobs from least favorite (1) to favorite (high number, depending on how long your list is.)

When everyone is finished making and ranking their list, discuss:

- What made your least favorite job so bad?

- What was it about your favorite job that made it such a good experience?

- What do your favorite jobs have in common? your least favorite?

■ The Issue

At its root, the word *vocation* comes from the Latin *vocationem* which literally means "a calling." The writer and pastor Frederick Buechner famously described *vocation,* saying "The place where God calls you to is the place where your deep gladness and the world's deep hunger meet."

In "The Original Puritan Work Ethic" Leland Ryken explains the "particular calling" in the Puritan doctrine of vocation. Ryken is clear to point out that "This view of work as vocation offers more than simply the possibility of serving God in one's daily work. It offers the possibility of serving God through or by means of that work. To work is to serve God."

- What do you see as the difference between a vocation and an occupation or a profession? Or should there be a difference at all? Explain.

- Do you consider the work you do to be your "calling" in life? Why or why not?

- What do you think is the difference between serving God in one's daily work and serving God through one's daily work?

■ Reflect

Take a moment to read Exodus 35:30–36:1 and Colossians 3:1–17 on your own. Jot down a few observations about the passages: What do these say about work? Are there any similar themes? In which ways do these passages connect with the Puritan idea of vocation?

■ Let's Explore

We should strive to live a God-centered life.

In his article, Ryken describes how the Puritans sought to put God first and value everything else in relation to God. "For the Puritans," he writes, "the God-centered life meant making the quest for spiritual and moral holiness the great business of life."

- What's your reaction to this Puritan sense of priorities and to their view of life as a quest for holiness? How does this compare or contrast with the way most Christians today view life?

Ryken goes on to quote Richard Baxter as saying, "In a divine commonwealth, holiness must have the principal honor and encouragement, and a great difference be made between the precious and the vile." Then, Ryken comments that "Our own culture has conspired to make such holiness seem burdensome, but the Puritans found it an appealing prospect."

- Do you tend to view holiness as burdensome or appealing? Why? In what ways does holiness seem burdensome in our culture?

Read Colossians 3:1–17. Here we find a holiness code that includes both "do's" and "do-not's."

- What would it look like, in the context of your specific job or career, to make holiness a central quest? Give specific examples based on this passage.

God calls us to our work.

Read Exodus 35:30–36:1. Here we read an example of the particular callings God gave to Bezalel and Oholiab as artists and craftsmen.

- What do you observe about God from this passage? What skills, abilities, or interests has God given to you?

Ryken explains that in the Puritan perspective, "A particular calling consists of the specific tasks and occupations that God places before a person in the course of daily living. It focuses on, but is not limited to, the work that a person does for a livelihood."

- Based on this understanding of vocation, what do you feel are your own particular callings? How do they relate to the work you do for your livelihood?

In *Keeping House: The Litany of Everyday Life*, Margaret Kim Peterson writes the following:

> One lifestyle magazine quotes a woman who said of a particular point in her life that she had decided from then on to spend as little time as possible "doing things that just don't matter." The result? "I haven't had my head inside a toilet since." I doubt, however, that this woman's toilet has gone uncleaned in the intervening years. I suspect someone else has been cleaning it, someone whose role in life, her employer imagines, is to do work that "doesn't matter."

- Have you ever felt like you were hired to do something that "doesn't matter"? How did it make you feel?

- The Puritan doctrine of vocation brings a sense of dignity to all sorts of work. How can we use this to transform our perspectives of "menial work"?

We should view all of our life as God's.

Ryken points out that for the Puritans "life was not divided into sacred and secular."

- In what ways do you tend to divide up your life between the sacred and the secular? What are the dangers of dividing life into two separate spheres?

- Imagine a cohesive life where everything is sacred (including your work). What does it look like? How is it different from the way you live now? What has changed: your circumstances or your attitudes?

Going Forward

Take a moment to review the sidebar from Richard Baxter's *A Christian Directory* in Ryken's article. Break into pairs and discuss two to three of the do's and do not's below that are directly applicable to you. Each topic includes an active commitment for the upcoming week.

"Be diligent in your callings, and spend no time in idleness and perform your labours with holy minds, to the glory of God, and in obedience to his commands."

- What does diligence in your calling look like?

- When are you tempted to spend time in idleness? What practical steps can you do to remedy this? Commit yourself to these steps this week.

"Take pleasure in your work, and then you will not be slothful in it."

- Do you take pleasure in your work? Why or why not?

- Is it possible to take pleasure in a job you detest? What are other options for you if this is the case? If you struggle with vocational angst, begin praying for and seeking new vocational options in your life.

"If God show you a way in which you may lawfully get more than in another way (without wrong to your soul, or to any other), if you refuse this, and then choose the less gainful way, you cross one of the ends of your calling, and you refuse to be God's steward."

- Despite the other things Baxter says about riches ("riches do make it much harder for a man to be saved") he includes this adage. Why, despite his warnings, do you think it was included?

- What is a right attitude toward monetary gain?

- Can vocation or calling include the goal of riches? Why or why not? If you struggle with your attitudes toward monetary gain, commit yourself to prayer about this in the upcoming week.

"You must not desire nor seek to get another's goods or labour for less than it is worth."

- What is the difference between being thrifty (or a good steward) and cheating someone out of fair wages?

- How does the contemporary economy bypass this directive?

- What are practical ways you can follow Baxter's advice? This week, try to understand the factors that influence price and seek fairness over bargains.

Once you and your partner have discussed several of Baxter's pieces of wisdom, pray about your commitments together.

■ Want to Explore More?

Recommended Resources

Want to explore this topic further? Here are some resources that will help.

Callings: Twenty Centuries of Christian Wisdom on Vocation, William C. Placher (Eerdmans, 2005; ISBN 0802829279)

The Complete Book of Everyday Christianity, Robert Banks and R. Paul Stevens (InterVarsity Press, 1997; ISBN 083081454X)

Keeping House: The Litany of Everyday Life, Margaret Kim Peterson (Jossey-Bass, 2007; ISBN 9780787976910)

Leading Lives That Matter: What We Should Do and Who We Should Be, Mark R. Schwehn and Dorothy C. Bass (Eerdmans, 2006; ISBN 9780802829313)

Redeeming the Time: A Christian Approach to Work and Leisure, Leland Ryken (Baker, 1995; ISBN 080105169X)

Notes

FAITH

How ambitious should Christians be?

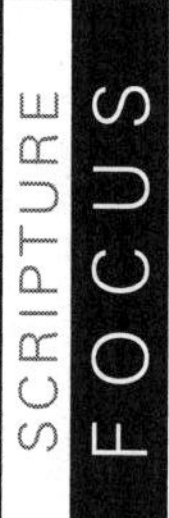

Proverbs 31:10–31

Mark 9:33–35, 10:35–45

Philippians 2:1–16

James 3:13–16

SESSION 3

THE DRIVE TO ACHIEVE

■

In today's success-oriented society, it's easy to be swept along in the surge up the corporate ladder. Is it acceptable for Christians to climb? Should Christians aim to be promoted, to achieve honors, and to become "great" in their arena of work? Didn't Jesus call us to seek to be the least, not the greatest?

This study will use John Throop's *Christianity Today* article "High Hopes: What's Wrong (and Right) with Ambition" to explore the question: are ambition and the Christian faith incompatible?

Before You Meet

Read "High Hopes: What's Wrong (and Right) with Ambition" by John Throop from *Christianity Today* magazine.

HIGH HOPES: WHAT'S WRONG (AND RIGHT) WITH AMBITION

by John Throop

"You certainly are ambitious!" the woman told me. Her tone of voice, facial expression, and bearing told me that it is wrong to be an ambitious Christian.

But are ambition and the urge to achieve each sinful traits that the godly Christian must abandon? Many Christians, especially those in the marketplace, cannot escape this question.

There appears to be an unwritten—and untested—assumption that ambition is incompatible with Christian faith. One text that pastors and teachers use to back this position is from the Book of James:

> Who is wise and understanding among you? Let him show it by his good life, by deeds done in the humility that comes from wisdom. But if you harbor bitter envy and selfish ambition in your hearts, do not boast about it or deny the truth. Such 'wisdom' does not come down from heaven but is earthly, unspiritual, of the devil. For where you have envy and selfish ambition, there you find disorder and every evil practice. (3:13–16, NIV)

But is *all* ambition selfish? Is *all* achievement carnal? If so, the faith is utterly irrelevant to the marketplace. Perhaps that is why so many Christians in business separate their work lives and their spiritual lives. The underlying attitudes and assumptions of the marketplace are alluring to those who are immersed in that system of values day in and day out. One stockbroker, a leader in his church, told me, "When I make my stock trades and deal in millions and millions, when I make money, I sometimes have to wonder, 'Can Jesus really be Lord of the marketplace?'"

The dissonance between the drive to achieve and the free grace of Jesus Christ can become acute for the sensitive Christian around promotion time. Ted, a thirty-three-year-old banker, was promoted to manage the loan department of a major Midwestern bank. It meant a $15,000 per year raise, a larger office, more support staff, greater responsibility, and direct decision-making authority. It was clear to Ted and his friends that he was on the fast track to the bank presidency.

But Ted felt torn. He said, "I feel guilty for working toward that position. Must it be sinful to want a higher position and work for it?"

Jesus: Lord of the Marketplace

We must test the assumption that faithfulness and ambition are contrary. If Jesus is Lord of all life, then he is Lord of the marketplace. Christian values must infuse and transform secular values such as ambition, achievement, competition, and the desire to excel.

The Christian can begin to discern the nature of unselfish ambition by becoming aware of the goals of that ambition, being able to state them honestly. God desires that we be truthful with ourselves about our inward attitudes and goals. But we need the guidance of God's Spirit as we test our ambition. We may discover that ambition does not *always* serve to glorify egos.

According to Ted Engstrom, president of World Vision International, "It all comes down to a matter of attitude. God frowns upon the man who is lazy and slothful—he has a lot to say about that in Scripture. The opposite of being lazy and slothful is to be aggressive, ambitious, and to do everything we can to honor the Lord in our living." As Engstrom says in *The Pursuit of Excellence,* "Striving for excellence in our work, whatever it is, is not only our Christian duty, but a basic form of Christian witness."

Thus the right use of ambition can reveal a God who made us in his creative and dynamic image. Ambition can be a way of honoring God and celebrating his purpose for life. Inward attitude is a key to ambition that is faithful both to God's intent for creation and to the call of the gospel.

Second, ambition can be faithful when exercised in concert with the ambition of others toward a common goal. The talents and abilities of others are brought forward along with one's own, and all benefit from the desire to excel. Teamwork is the key concept, and service to and with others is the norm.

"Ambition is good if a person uses it for the common good of every one with whom they work," says Frederick F. Broda, a vice-president of Swiss Bancorporation and a leader in his church. "The way we channel ambition, which I think is a good Christian witness as well, is to foster a team spirit. Everybody gets credit if there's success."

In a team effort, each member realizes that his well-being and achievement is tied to that of others. Individual abilities are called out and improved only in relation to others using their gifts for a common goal. Similarly, the apostles and the disciples of the early church worked as a team to promote the gospel of Christ and to build the church in his name. They were not out for their own advancement, but for the good of one another and the kingdom.

Faithful Ambition

Faithful ambition is to be a servant. Engstrom believes that is the key to Christian witness in the marketplace.

"Even for a Christian in business, there has to be a servant heart," he says. Yet the presence of ego makes the blend of ambition and servanthood tenuous indeed. Executives admit it is difficult to be a leader and maintain a servant attitude.

Since leaders are often in positions where they can be served, rather than serve, there can be a spiritual conflict between the drive to achieve and the gospel call to serve. The disciples James and John wanted to ascend to positions of power and influence in the kingdom of God, where Jesus would reign. But Jesus called all of his disciples together to tell them, "You know that those who are regarded as rulers of the Gentiles lord it over them, and their high officials exercise authority over them. Not so with you. Instead, whoever wants to become great among you must be your servant, and whoever wants to be first must be slave of all" (Mark 10:42–44, NIV).

The specter of Jesus's certain death on the cross loomed over this passage. To understand that position of leadership you want, you must understand the cup that I must drink, said Jesus. If you want to be ambitious and excel as my follower, you must be prepared not only to serve, but also to suffer.

Ambition, if it is to be true to the gospel, must be purified in the fire of suffering. Ambition's true purpose is not merely to achieve our own ends or to perfect our own gifts. Rather, it is to witness to the power of God to mend broken lives and rekindle the desire to live creatively and fully. Only then can one achieve and excel in a way that does not have self-exaltation as its first priority. Although one ought not seek the painful, ambition may bring suffering as well as success. Service, the principal orientation of the ambitious Christian, is surely not the easy way to climb the ladder.

The Ambitious Christian

Christian ambition seeks not only to maximize one's God-given potential, but to call out the potential in others. The ambitious Christian realizes that positions of power and influence are not to be sought after for glamour and glory. Rather, the ambitious Christian will find the awe of responsibility and the pain of decision—suffering that a Christian can accept, relying on the power of God.

Ambition and competition are transformed from marketplace values to supremely Christian values when they are directed to the raising up of others. In that way, the Christian gives God glory. As the apostle Paul says of Christ's ambition,

> Your attitude should be the same as that of Christ Jesus: Who, being in very nature God, did not consider equality with God a thing to be grasped, but made himself nothing, taking the very nature of a servant, being made in human likeness. And being found in appearance as a man, he humbled himself and became obedient to death—even death on a cross! Therefore God exalted him to the highest place and gave him the name that is above every name, that at the name of Jesus every knee should bow, in heaven and on earth and under the earth, and every tongue confess that Jesus Christ is Lord, to the glory of God the Father. (Phil. 2:5–11, NIV)

The ambitious Christian strives after the example of Christ, whose ambition was to serve; who, in serving, suffered; who, in suffering, was exalted. Then, and only then, can our ambition be God's exaltation—hardly a small, selfish, human goal.

The Rev. Dr. John R. Throop is president of The Summit Planning Group, a consulting and training firm based in Peoria, Illinois. He also is on the staff of LaSalle County Episcopal Ministry, a four-church parish based in Streator, Illinois. He is the author of two books, Shape Up from the Inside Out (Tyndale House Publishers) and Dealing with Suicide (David C. Cook). ("High Hopes: What's Wrong (and Right) with Ambition" was originally published in Christianity Today, *October 3, 1986).*

■ Open Up

Select one of these activities to launch your discussion time.

Option 1

Discuss one of these icebreaker questions:

- Share about a time you achieved or accomplished something you're proud of.

- Do you generally enjoy or dislike competition? Why?

- Does competition bring out the best in you . . . or the worst? Explain.

Option 2

Play multiple rounds of “Rock, Paper, Scissors” or another simple, competitive game. (If you’re able, include fun prizes for the winners!) After the game, talk about these questions:

- Do you like competitive games? If so, what are your favorites? If not, why not?

- Did this game bring out character traits in group members that you don’t normally see? How did your “competition” personality match up with your normal personality?

- What are some ambitions you have in life, particularly in the work you do? What goals would you like to accomplish in the coming years?

■ The Issue

In his article, Throop recalled an experience he once had: "'You certainly are ambitious!' the woman told me. Her tone of voice, facial expression, and bearing told me that it is wrong to be an ambitious Christian."

Throop goes on to wonder, "[A]re ambition and the urge to achieve each sinful traits that the godly Christian must abandon? Many Christians, especially those in the marketplace, cannot escape this question."

- What are some reasons Christians assume that ambition is incompatible with Christian faith? Which of these reasons seem valid and which do not?

■ Reflect

Take a moment on your own to read Proverbs 31:10–31; Mark 9:33–35, 10:35–45; Philippians 2:1–16; and James 3:13–16. Jot down a few notes and observations about the passages: What do these passages say about ambition, competition, or the drive to achieve? What different perspectives do these passages offer? What questions or issues do these passages raise for you?

■ Let's Explore

Selfish ambition has no place in the Christian life.
Read Mark 9:33–35 and 10:35–45.

- It's easy to point fingers at the disciples for their repeated focus on self-advancement—but what about us? How does this desire for greatness pop up in the lives of modern Christians?

- Do you think it's wrong or sinful to desire individual recognition? Why or why not?

In his article, Throop mentions James 3:13–16 as a passage that leads Christians to assume ambition is incompatible with Christian living. Read the passage in your own Bible, then consider this paraphrase of it from *The Message*:

> Do you want to be counted wise, to build a reputation for wisdom? Here's what you do: Live well, live wisely, live humbly. It's the way you live, not the way you talk, that counts. Mean-spirited ambition isn't wisdom. Boasting that you are wise isn't wisdom. Twisting the truth to make yourselves sound wise isn't wisdom. It's the furthest thing from wisdom—it's animal cunning, devilish conniving. Whenever you're trying to look better than others or get the better of others, things fall apart and everyone ends up at the others' throats.

- In what ways is ambition selfish? How can competitiveness be mean-spirited? Share an example of a time you observed others acting this way—or describe a time when you were selfishly ambitious or mean-spirited in a competitive situation.

- What are the specific attitudes and behaviors condemned in James 3:13–16 and the passages in Mark? Do these passages suggest that ambition is incompatible with the Christian life? Defend your answer.

Ambition can honor God.

- What may happen in our lives when we believe ambition is sinful? How could this belief affect one's work or one's relationship with co-workers in positive or negative ways? How would this affect the work you do in your job or daily tasks?

A pragmatist would suggest that ambition and competitiveness are necessary in our world—without them, there'd be disastrous consequences. Products would be poor in quality, the workforce would become lazy, businesses would fall apart, the economy would collapse, and there wouldn't be innovations in technology or medicine, just to name a few. In a practical sense, some believe, ambition is both good and necessary.

- What are other practical and positive purposes for ambition and competition? What right uses of ambition for the Christian does Throop mention in his article?

Read Proverbs 31:10–31.

- Would you describe this woman as ambitious? Why or why not? What other adjectives would you use to describe her?

- What might it look like if this woman were in your job or did your daily work? In what ways do you think she'd be ambitious? What achievements would she aim for—and why?

In his article, Throop says, "the right use of ambition can reveal a God who made us in his creative and dynamic image. Ambition can be a way of honoring God and celebrating his purpose for life."

- How do we reflect the nature of God when we are ambitious? How does God-honoring ambition contrast with selfish ambition? Give some examples.

Christian values can transform ambition.

Christ is our ultimate example of humility, meekness, and selflessness. But in our modern world, these traits are often misunderstood and carry connotations of weakness and passivity. Does humility really mean a lack of ambition? Does meekness mean being a doormat for others to walk upon? Does selflessness mean giving up all our own dreams and goals?

Christ not only modeled humility—he also modeled ambition. Christ's meekness didn't represent a *lack* of ambition, but rather it revealed a *different* ambition.

Read Philippians 2:1–16.

- What stands out to you most from this passage? According to this passage, what was Christ's ambition? What was Paul's ambition? What should be our ambition?

Throop states that "faithful ambition is to be a servant."

- How can one be ambitious and still demonstrate a servant-like attitude? Explore what this would look like in the context of your own daily work.

Throop remarks that, "Christian values must infuse and transform secular values such as ambition, achievement, competition, and the desire to excel."

- Do you think all of these values can be transformed and lived out in the Christian life? Discuss each of these values together, contrasting what they look like in the secular realm with what they'd mean transformed in the life of a Christian:

- Ambition

- Achievement

- Competition

- The desire to excel

■ Going Forward

Break into pairs to discuss the next two questions:

Throop quotes Ted Engstrom as saying that "striving for excellence in our work, whatever it is, is not only our Christian duty, but a basic form of Christian witness."

- How can you demonstrate Christ's love to others by doing your best? How can others see Christ in you by the way you do the specific tasks required in your daily work?

In his article, Throop remarks that, "The Christian can begin to discern the nature of unselfish ambition by becoming aware of the goals of that ambition, being able to state them honestly."

- Review with your partner one or two of the personal ambitions and goals you shared at the beginning of the study. Honestly evaluate together the reasons for those ambitions: Are they Christ-like and God-honoring? Are they selfish? If so, can they be transformed?

Gather back together as a group and discuss this quote:

> Be always displeased with what you are, if you desire to attain to what you art not; for where you have pleased yourself, there you abide! But if you say, I have enough, you perish. Always add, always walk, always proceed. Neither stand still, nor go back, nor deviate.
>
> —Augustine

- What new "ambition" do you have in light of this study? Share with the group how you feel inspired to grow or change with God's help.

As a concluding prayer, meditatively listen as a group member reads aloud Philippians 2:5–11, then pray silently together, each one inviting God to help you develop a servant attitude in your work and to fill you with ambition to do your best in your work for his glory.

■ Want to Explore More?

Recommended Resources

Want to explore this topic further? Here are some resources that will help.

The Crucifixion of Ministry: Surrendering Our Ambitions to the Service of Christ, Andrew Purves (InterVarsity Press, 2007; ISBN 0830834397)

A Guide to Christian Ambition: Using Career, Politics, and Culture to Influence the World, Hugh Hewitt (Thomas Nelson, 2006; ISBN 0785288716)

Be Last: Descending to Greatness, Jeremy Kingsley (Tyndale, 2008; ISBN 1414316410)

Descending Into Greatness, Bill Hybels and Rob Wilkins (Zondervan, 1994; ISBN 0310544718)

Forgetting Ourselves on Purpose: Vocation and the Ethics of Ambition, Brian J. Mahan and Robert Coles (Jossey-Bass, 2002; ISBN 0787956333)

Holy Ambition: What it Takes to Make a Difference for God, Chip Ingram (Moody Publishers, 2002; ISBN 0802429785)

Notes

FAITH

In an age of titles, do you know who you are in Christ?

1 Samuel 6:1–13

Luke 9:23–25

Philippians 1:20–22a

2 Thessalonians 3:6–15

SESSION 4

DOES WHAT I "DO" = WHO I AM?

■

"What do you do?" is often the very first question we ask when meeting someone new. But does a person's job have anything to do with who they really are? Within our current culture, where the quest for power and prestige reigns supreme, is it even possible to be defined by something other than our job title, house, car, or investment portfolio?

Our jobs can positively connect to our identities and serve as a perfect expression of the passions, giftings, and interests God has placed within us. However, there is also danger in placing one's sense of significance in one's job. After all, if your job is your identity, what would you do if you found yourself suddenly unemployed? Who would you be?

Using Steve Jolley's *Christianity Today* article "Don't Ask Me What I 'Do,'" we'll look at some of the core issues of identity, our jobs as temporal labor, and the calling of Christians to encourage the body of Christ.

Before You Meet

Read "Don't Ask Me What I 'Do'" by Steve Jolley from *Christianity Today* magazine.

DON'T ASK ME WHAT I "DO"

We need to define ourselves in Christ rather than by our jobs.

by Steve Jolley

When I go to a party, meet a neighbor, or am introduced to anyone, the inevitable question rears its ugly head: "What do you do?" I resent that question. "Who are you?" or "What are your interests?" would be better questions. To be defined by how I earn my living bothers me.

In our society, work defines who we are. Work is no longer just work; it is an extension of our very being. No longer do we have jobs; we have "careers." No longer do people find satisfaction in providing for their families; they now need "fulfillment" from their work. Some, the unlucky ones, even feel they have found "meaning" in their places of employment. For these, salvation is found in a well-placed résumé.

This is a sad state of affairs for anyone, but especially for Christians, who should be defined by their relationship to Christ.

Christians who allow their employment to define them become trapped in hierarchies of power, prestige, and pedigree. The pernicious effects on the unity of the body of Christ, especially in its local manifestation, are pronounced. All too often, leadership in a local church is based upon financial success, rather than spiritual maturity.

Consider how often we find that serving on a church board or in other positions of leadership is contingent upon accomplishment in the workplace. Further, consider how many local churches take pride in the number of community leaders who are members.

I understand why so many people seek "fulfillment" or "meaning" in their jobs. Jobs can meet legitimate ego needs. But Christians—who ought to know better—are meeting their primary needs for self-esteem, meaning, and fulfillment in their jobs, rather than through kingdom ministry. The vast majority of Christians spend more emotional energy compiling a business plan than in laying strategies to affect the world for Christ. They find more personal satisfaction if their sales figures are up than if their next-door neighbor responds to the gospel. They somehow feel more "secure" after they have received a raise than because they have been raised with Christ.

The Temporal and the Eternal

There are at least two critical reasons why this troublesome scenario exists:

First, Christians have failed to distinguish between temporal and eternal labor. The purpose of temporal labor is clearly seen in Scripture. For example, Paul says, "If any one does not provide for his relatives, and especially for his own family, he has disowned the faith and is worse than an unbeliever" (1 Tim. 5:8). Paul again affirms the value of temporal labor in Ephesians 4:28: "Let the thief no longer steal, but rather let him labor, doing honest work with his hands, so that he may be able to give to those in need." Temporal labor is good and has value in that, at minimum, it provides for the physical needs of ourselves and others. With Calvin and the other Reformers, we must strongly assert that temporal labor is good and ordained by God at Creation. However, our temporal labor must be understood in relation to our eternal labor.

Scripture delineates the value of eternal labor. In evaluating his own life, Paul muses on his reason for being: "For to me to live is Christ, and to die is gain. If it is to be life in the flesh, that means fruitful labor for me" (Phil. 1:21–22a).

Put simply, labor has value when we know its purpose. When Christians confuse temporal labor with eternal labor, there is a distinct probability that temporal labor will begin to usurp the place of kingdom work.

Stroking Egos

Second, Christians place an inappropriate amount of importance on their jobs because of their real needs for self-esteem. Secular employers have done a better job of stroking ego needs than most local churches. Compare the salesman who makes the big sale and receives both hearty congratulations from higher-ups and a hefty check for the effort, to the Christian who faithfully leads a Bible study, shares Christ with a neighbor, or disciples a brother or sister. Business offers immediate, tangible rewards, while the church lets labor go unnoticed and unrewarded. Add the meeting of ego needs to the tremendous importance our culture places on what you "do," and it is little wonder that Christians have such difficulty distinguishing the relative value of temporal and eternal labor.

I am not worried because believers find importance in their jobs. I am worried by the inappropriate amount of importance that work occupies in the Christian life. At life's end, I don't want to be like the disgruntled writer of Ecclesiastes, "So I . . . gave my heart up to despair over all the toil of my labors under the sun" (2:20). I want to find meaning in my life in Christ, not in my sales figures or corporate status. I want to find my primary needs for self-esteem and fulfillment met through service to the risen Lord.

Steve Jolley is Teaching Pastor at Santa Barbara Community Church in California. This article originally appeared in Christianity Today.

■ Open Up

Select one of these activities to launch your discussion time.

Option 1

Discuss one of these icebreaker questions:

- Think back to when you were a little kid. What did you want to be when you "grew up?" What other career dreams did you have as you grew through your childhood and teen years?

- When you shared your childhood dreams with your family or friends, what were their responses?

- In what ways are you following some of those dreams you had as a little kid? In what ways is your life different now?

Option 2

When we observe people, we often think we know everything about them simply based upon what we see (what clothes they're wearing, what they're driving, and so on). Others often think that they know *us* merely by our outward appearance.

Look through a collection of magazines and newspapers. Each of you should choose a picture of someone that you think you can describe to the other members of your group. (Do not select a celebrity who you already know about—select a photograph of someone you don't know.)

Based upon his or her outward appearance alone, try to describe what this person is like to the group. What do you think this person does for a living? How successful do you think this person is? What do you think he or she is passionate about? What do you guess this person's personality is like? In what areas do you think this person is most gifted?

After you've all had a turn, talk about this question together:

- If someone saw your picture in a magazine, would they be able to accurately tell who you really are? What might they assume about you? What aspects of who you are might they miss? Explain.

The Issue

- What kinds of assumptions—both positive and negative—have others made about you based on what you "do"? Were their assumptions accurate?

In "Don't Ask Me What I 'Do,'" Steve Jolley contends, "In our society, work defines who we are. Work is no longer just work; it is an extension of our very being."

- Do you think work should be "just work," separate from issues of identity? Or do you feel your work is deeply connected with who you are? Explain.

Reflect

Take a moment to read 1 Samuel 6:1–13, Luke 9:23–25, Philippians 1:20–22a, and 2 Thessalonians 3:6–15 on your own. Write down your own observations about the passages: What words, phrases, or images stand out to you most? What insights do these passages give you about the place of work in one's identity? What questions do these passages bring up?

Let's Explore

Identity: What (or Who) defines you?

- When someone asks you "What do you do?," do you like answering the question? What feelings does it evoke? Confidence? Joy? Pride? Low self-esteem? Embarrassment? Shame? Explain.

Jolley articulates his disdain for the question, "What do you do?" and urges us to consider questions that are more broad. He argues that "Who are you?" or "What are your interests?" would be significantly better options.

- How would you like to answer these types of questions? What other questions do you think might be good ways to get to know more about others you meet?

In 1 Samuel 16:1–13, God sends Samuel to anoint the next king of Israel. Read this passage.

- Consider each of the main human players in this account—Samuel, Jesse, Eliab (and the other older brothers), and David. Which of these people do you most relate to? Why? Can you see a bit of yourself in each of them? Explain.

- Is Samuel doing something wrong here or just something natural? Explain.

- How does it make you feel to know that God looks at your heart? Do you think "external" factors in your life—such as your job, your appearance, or your outward personality—are important to God? If so, to what degree? If not, why not?

- Jolley asserts, "Christians who allow their employment to define them become trapped in hierarchies of power, prestige, and pedigree." How can intertwining personal identity and employment be dangerous? Share from your own experience.

- Imagine how you'd feel if you suddenly lost your job. How might that impact your sense of identity? (If you've gone through a period of unemployment, consider sharing with the group how that experience affected your sense of self.)

Temporal vs. Eternal Labor: Where are you placing your effort?

In his article, Jolley draws a line between temporal labor (the work we do for a paycheck) with eternal labor (the work we do for the kingdom of God). Read some of Paul's comments on temporal labor in 2 Thessalonians 3:6–15.

- What emphasis does this passage place on the importance of temporal labor? In what other ways can temporal labor be important in the life of a Christian?

In his article, Jolley bemoans how "Christians have failed to distinguish between temporal and eternal labor." Yet others, such as theologian

Dorothy Sayers, promote a different viewpoint, asserting that everyday work should *not* be viewed separately from eternally focused work. Consider Sayers' comment in her essay "Why Work?": "[The Church] has forgotten that the secular vocation is sacred. . . . Let the Church remember this: that every maker and worker is called to serve God *in* his profession or trade—not outside."

- Do you think there is a difference between temporal and eternal labor? Why or why not? Which perspective best represents the way you normally view your work on an average day?

- What could be the danger of taking either viewpoint to an extreme? Give examples.

In his article, Jolley points out one of the dangers, saying "When Christians confuse temporal labor with eternal labor, there is a distinct probability that temporal labor will begin to usurp the place of kingdom work." He goes on to say that "I am not worried because believers find importance in their jobs. I am worried by the inappropriate amount of importance that work occupies in the Christian life."

- Do you know Christians who seem so focused on their work that they neglect to put passion, effort, or focus into "kingdom work" such as evangelism, personal spiritual growth, or caring for the needy? What are their lives like?

- How do Jolley's words of caution apply to you? When have you placed too much importance on your work to the detriment of your focus on spiritual pursuits?

■ Going Forward

Read Philippians 1:20–22a. In our world that sizes up people based on their jobs—that urges people to seek after self-fulfillment, pride, and meaning in the arena of career—Paul's words stand in sharp contrast. Paul's focus wasn't on himself; it was squarely on Christ.

- What strikes you most about Paul's words here? How does this passage relate to the issues we've discussed so far in this study?

Take a few moments for personal reflection as you each privately read Jesus's words in Luke 9:23–25 and individually reflect on the next two questions.

- We are called to find our ultimate meaning in Christ—not our career. How do these passages challenge you personally about the degree of importance you place on your work?

- How do these passages challenge you about the degree of importance you place on your *self*?

Form pairs and take some time to share candidly about ways you've felt challenged during this study. Identify one area of "kingdom work" in which you feel called to devote greater energy and focus. Then pray aloud for each other, asking God to help your partner find his or her true identity in Christ alone.

■ Want to Explore More?

Recommended Resources

Want to explore this topic further? Here are some resources that will help.

Books

If You Want To Walk on Water: You've Got to Get Out of the Boat, John Ortberg (Zondervan, 2001; ISBN: 0-310-22863-8)

Let Your Life Speak: Listening for the Voice of Vocation, Parker J. Palmer (Jossey-Bass, 2000; ISBN: 0-7879-4735-0)

The Oak Inside the Acorn, Max Lucado (Tommy Nelson, 2006; ISBN-13: 978-1-4003-0601-5)

The Search for Significance—Seeing Your True Worth Through God's Eyes, Robert S McGee (Thomas Nelson, 2003; ISBN 0849944244)

Waking the Dead: The Glory of a Heart Fully Alive, John Eldredge (Thomas Nelson, 2003; ISBN: 0-7852-6553-8)

When the Game is Over, It all Goes Back in the Box, John Ortberg (Zondervan, 2007; ISBN-13: 978-0-310-25350-1)

DVD

Nooma, 008, Dust, Rob Bell, (Flannel/Zondervan, 2004; ISBN: 0-310-26527-4)

Web

"Making Career Decisions Within God's Will for Your Life," http://www.christiancareercenter.com/guidance/adecison.shtml

What does it look like to be a witness in the workplace?

Matthew 28:16–20

Acts 1:7–9

1 Thessalonians 4:11–12

SESSION 5

THE 9-TO-5 WINDOW

■

Imagine Joe Christian. He's so enthusiastic about his faith that he can't stop talking about Jesus, even at work. He mentions Jesus by name during meetings. He quotes Bible verses at the lunch table. He surreptitiously sneaks WWJD bracelets into office mailboxes. He even posts fliers for after-work prayer meetings in the bathroom stalls. In the process, he's succeeded in alienating or offending a majority of his co-workers.

Now imagine Fred Christian. He loves Jesus passionately, but he has a strong sense of duty and loyalty when it comes to his job. So as not to offend others, he hardly *ever* talks about God when he's on the clock (though he has been known to say "Merry Christmas" to co-workers each December). He's honest and hard-working and well-liked. But no one at work has a clue about his religious beliefs.

Now imagine a new movement—one that views one's career field as both an arena for excellence and for ministry. Os Hillman calls it "workplace ministry" and he defines it this way: having "an intentional focus on equipping men and women in all spheres of work and society to understand and experience their work and life as a holy calling from God."

In this study we'll look at "Ministry @ Work" by Penny Schlaf Musco from *Today's Christian Woman* as you explore how God may be calling you to be a witness in the workplace.

■ Before You Meet

Read "Ministry @ Work" By Penny Schlaf Musco from *Today's Christian Woman* magazine.

MINISTRY @ WORK

Any job can be an outreach—it's all in your attitude.

by Penny Schlaf Musco

Jose Zeilstra grew up in a church that focused on sending people overseas to share the gospel. "The feeling was if you're a true Christian, you go into full-time ministry; the business world wasn't a place for real believers," she says. Jose admits she rebelled against this mindset, eventually reaching the position of vice president at JPMorgan Chase. But it wasn't until she read *Roaring Lambs* by Bob Briner, a book in which Briner argues that Christians should be salt and light in all arenas of life, that she finally realized her career was a legitimate calling from God. "The first time I spoke publicly about my faith was for *Fortune* magazine," she says. "In the business world, it doesn't get more public than that." She connects her two worlds by attending and speaking at Bible studies and workplace seminars in Manhattan, as well as meeting regularly with a Christian mentor and a group of spiritually like-minded CEOs.

Angie Tracey's revelation came at a women's event. "I'd seen the value of the National Prayer Breakfast and other prayer gatherings when I worked in Washington, D.C. So when I started working at the Centers for Disease Control and Prevention (CDC) in Atlanta, I felt strongly that our agency could benefit from having similar meetings. I immediately started praying God would bring someone to lead them." Then, while at a women's conference, the Holy Spirit told Angie *she* was that leader.

"I was going to send an e-mail inviting our employees to a breakfast or lunch," says Angie. "I thought maybe I'd have ten or fifteen people respond, twenty if I was truly blessed." She quickly discovered that to use the CDC's e-mail system for this kind of solicitation, she had to establish an employee association. So Angie tackled the detailed forms and the bureaucratic layers typical of an agency with nearly ten thousand employees in ten states. She prayed every step of the way, and to her amazement, what should have taken a year took two weeks start to finish. The first ever official Christian employee association in the federal government was born.

Within hours of approval, Angie received more than two hundred e-mails and phone calls. Six days later, planes crashed into the World Trade Center. She believes God was preparing the agency to handle the extra stress from 9/11 and the war on terror. The first meeting attracted 225 employees; now the CDC Christian Fellowship Group has more than five hundred members.

Jose and Angie would be the first to say they're not doing anything special. They've realized they don't have to separate their faith from their vocation; they're missionaries right where they are.

Everything Old Is New Again

Bringing God to work is often referred to as workplace or worklife ministry. Os Hillman, director of the International Coalition of Workplace Ministries, defines it as "an intentional focus on equipping men and women in all spheres of work and society to understand and experience their work and life as a holy calling from God." Os points out that Jesus spent the majority of his life as a carpenter, not as a preacher; 122 of Jesus's 132 public appearances were in the marketplace, and forty-five of the fifty-two parables are set in a work environment.

Dr. Bob Reccord, former president of the North American Mission Board of the Southern Baptist Convention and author of *Made to Count: Discovering What to Do With Your Life*, indicates that although the Hebrew word *avodah* is the root word of both work and worship, the Reformation effectively separated the world into two classes: secular and sacred. This split led to what Os sees as a "hierarchy of calling" within the church: "We said the most spiritual vocation is the pastor, then the missionary, then the full-time Christian worker, and then the stay-at-home mom, and way down at the bottom is the ad agency executive or the nurse. It's often an unspoken hierarchy, but it's there."

But when you read the Scriptures, you never find culture referred to as secular and sacred. "God literally intended for everything to have a sacred touch," says Bob. So while he doesn't intend to diminish the importance of pastors and missionaries, he seeks to raise the church's view of the calling to workplace ministries.

Preach Not

The path from vision for workplace ministry to concrete action isn't always clear. As Jack Munday of the Billy Graham Evangelistic Association emphasizes, "We're not encouraging people to go to work on Monday and start preaching." Instead, he says Christians must change the way we view our job, to see it not only as the place where we make our living, but where we consciously live out eternal values. That kind of perspective, he insists, can't help but positively impact the people with whom we spend the majority of our time.

"We hear a lot about the church's involvement in city transformation today, but we've not seen one city transformed in America," says Os Hillman. "The reason is that we haven't equipped, empowered, and affirmed those in the marketplace who have the ability and authority to make changes in the cities and in our culture." If there's going to be real revival in the nation, he believes it will come through Christians purposefully bringing their faith into this "9-to-5 window."

Linda Rios Brooks couldn't agree more. She's the author of *Frontline Christians in a Bottom-Line World* and president of the Lakeland Leadership League, which, among other things, ministers to the Colorado Springs community by providing affordable housing. "The kingdom is going to advance through commerce, science, the arts, and education," she says. "If all we ever tell people is that to be really holy you've got to have a job in the church, we're going to continue to forfeit our influence in those areas."

Angie knows how tough it can be to balance working for her earthly bosses and for the heavenly Boss. After a few employees took issue with her Christian fellowship group, the CDC reexamined the separation of church and state issues involved. "That's when I had to become quite an expert on the matter," she laughs. Her favorite tool is a set of guidelines released by the Clinton administration on respecting religious practices within the federal workplace. "It's amazing how much we employees can do and how little we Christians know about it," she says.

"Most groups are well aware that you can't force your religion on another employee," Angie adds. "As Christians, we wouldn't want to do that." Case in point: At the CDC, an atheist employee sent her a "venomous" e-mail blasting the Christian fellowship group. After much prayer, Angie replied graciously, addressing the legal concerns, and the woman backed off. About a month later, the woman sent her another e-mail: "'I thought you might want to know I was visiting one of our facilities and the Christian Fellowship Group there was having their Christmas party. I went for the first time, sang Christmas carols, and thought of you.'"

Like any good businesswoman, Angie keeps her eye on the bottom line: "I believe God equips us with certain skills to do the kind of job he has for us to do for society. But I also believe that as Christians we're ambassadors for the kingdom of God, and that's our job too."

Penny Schlaf Musco lives and works in New Jersey. ("Ministry @ Work" was originally published in Today's Christian Woman, *July/August 2007, Vol. 29, No. 4, Page 54)*

■ Open Up

Select one of these activities to launch your discussion time.

Option 1

Discuss one of these icebreaker questions:

- Who is your closest friend at work? Why? What do you and your co-worker have in common?

- Who is someone in your workplace you admire? In what ways does he or she inspire you?

- Are there people at your work who rub you the wrong way? Without naming names, describe what annoys you or frustrates you about that person.

Option 2

Watch a few minutes from an episode of the TV show *The Office.* Select a segment of the show that depicts several characters from the show interacting with one another. (Preview it to make sure it's a "clean" segment!) Then talk about these questions:

- Are any of these characters similar to people you work with? Have you ever been in a workplace situation like this? Explain.

- Have you ever had to work with someone who was obnoxious or extremely annoying? Without naming names, describe what annoyed you about that person.

■ The Issue

Some non-Christians view Christian efforts to witness in the workplace—praying in the lunchroom, evangelizing, or decorating one's cubicle with Christian posters and Bible verses—as obnoxious and annoying.

- Do you think this judgment is fair? Why or why not? In what ways can Christians come across as obnoxious?

In an interview on www.faithintheworkplace.com, David Miller, once a top executive in the banking world and now the executive director of the Yale Center for Faith and Culture, remarked about how Christian efforts to witness at work can often be received badly by coworkers. He said, "Such expression of overt religiosity seems insincere or like sloganeering. So many just decide to side-step the faith question, shutting down for fear of offending someone . . . But there's a difference between obnoxious harassment and an attractive life of faith."

- In your opinion, what's the difference between "obnoxious" Christian witnessing in the workplace and living an "attractive life of faith"? Share specific examples of each type of behavior that you've observed in your work.

■ Reflect

Take a moment on your own to read Matthew 28:16–20, Acts 1:7–9, and 1 Thessalonians 4:11–12. Jot down a few notes and observations about the passages: What do these passages say about evangelism and what it should—or shouldn't—involve? What do you see as the key issues in these passages? What questions do these passages raise for you?

■ Let's Explore

Your workplace is your mission field.

In his interview, David Miller observed, "Fewer than 10 percent of regular churchgoers, surveys say, can remember the last time their pastor preached on the topic of work. When he or she did preach on work, inevitably the tone was critical—if not hostile—and painted all business people as greedy and uncaring." And Os Hillman, director of the International

Coalition of Workplace Ministries, notes that he's observed an "unspoken hierarchy" in the way Christians view various careers—some as more spiritually significant than others.

- Describe the unspoken hierarchy you've observed in your church or Christian experience: What careers seem to be perceived as most important or significant? Which are in the middle? Which careers seem to be viewed as least spiritually significant—or may even be viewed negatively by the church?

- Imagine viewing your current job as "full-time ministry" or considering yourself as a missionary to your workplace. Would the label fit? What would be different in your mind-set or actions if you treated your job this way?

Read Acts 1:7–9. Now re-read it a second time, each group member adding his or her place of employment in the blank below:

"You will be my witnesses—in Jerusalem, in all of Judea, in Samaria, in______________, and in every part of the world."

- What's your reaction to hearing the passage this way? Do you think it is in line with Jesus's intended meaning? Why or why not?

Your actions are a powerful witness.

In her article, Musco includes Jack Munday's clarification of what workplace ministry should—and should not—look like. He said, "We're not encouraging people to go to work on Monday and start preaching." Instead, we should view our workplace as an arena in which "we consciously live out eternal values."

- What "eternal values" are most lacking—and most needed—in your workplace? What are specific ways you could consciously embody those values? Brainstorm ideas and examples together.

Read 1 Thessalonians 4:11–12. Some find this passage problematic. After all, it seems to suggest that Christians should keep to themselves entirely. But does this passage really discourage evangelism?

- What do you think? What avenues of evangelism does this passage encourage? What would this look like in modern terms?

You've probably heard this famous quotation, often attributed to St. Francis of Assisi: "Preach the gospel at all times. If necessary, use words."

- Have you known someone who's been a profound "preacher" of the gospel—but without words? Someone whose demeanor, actions, and behavior have powerfully pointed to Jesus? Describe that person and what stands out to you most about him or her.

- What would it look like for you to "preach the gospel" without words in your workplace? Who do you feel most called to "preach" to?

God may also call you to witness in the workplace through challenging words and bold actions.

Some understand 1 Thessalonians 4:11–12 and the quote attributed to St. Francis to imply that verbally sharing the gospel is not necessary. In fact, at first glance, the command to mind our business seems to let us off the hook when it comes to evangelism!

- What's your response to this idea? Is a witness of actions and behavior sufficient? Or must we "use words" as well? Explain.

- Musco's article highlighted several examples of Christian efforts to witness in the workplace through both words and action. Which story stood out to you the most? Why?

Read Matthew 28:16–20. Making disciples and teaching others are both aspects of witnessing that obviously necessitate using words. But speaking overtly about Jesus in the context of a secular workplace can feel like navigating a field of landmines!

- How receptive is your workplace environment to overt religious expression? What negative consequences might you face for talking openly about your faith or promoting Christian practices like prayer?

- When it comes to your verbal witness, how do you draw the line between what's appropriate and inappropriate for the workplace? Explain.

■ Going Forward

Linda Rios Brooks, author of *Frontline Christians in a Bottom-Line World,* said, "The kingdom is going to advance through commerce, science, the arts, and education. If all we ever tell people is that to be really holy you've got to have a job in the church, we're going to continue to forfeit our influence in those areas."

- What's the danger of Christians living without a missional perspective on the workplace? What examples can you cite of arenas in which it appears that Christians have forfeited our influence?

Break into pairs to talk about this final question:

In her article, Musco cites Os Hillman, the director of the International Coalition of Workplace Ministries, and his passion to see "Christians purposefully bringing their faith into this '9-to-5 window.'"

- How do you feel God personally challenging you to be purposeful in bringing your faith to the "9-to-5 window"? How is he speaking to you in the area of the values you model, the actions you take, and the words you speak?

Musco also describes Angie Tracey's efforts to begin a fellowship group at her work. She quotes Angie as saying, "I believe God equips us with certain skills to do the kind of job he has for us to do for society. But I also believe that as Christians we're ambassadors for the kingdom of God, and that's our job too." Pray in pairs, asking God to help your partner fulfill his or her "job requirements" as a kingdom ambassador when he or she goes to work tomorrow.

■ Want to Explore More?

Recommended Resources

Want to explore this topic further? Here are some resources that will help.

Organizations and Internet Resources

International Coalition of Workplace Ministries, www.icwm.net, (678) 455-6262

His Church at Work, www.hischurchatwork.org, (404) 935-5757

WorkPlace Influence, www.workplaceinfluence.org, (719) 548-1123

InterVarsity's Ministry in Daily Life, www.ivmdl.org, (608) 274-4823

Guidelines on Religious Exercise and Religious Expression in the Federal Workplace, http://clinton2.nara.gov/WH/New/html/19970819-3275.html

"Silicon Valley Saints" by Tony Carnes, *Christianity Today,* http://www.christianitytoday.com/ct/2001/august6/1.34.html

"Interview with David Miller," Nancy Lovell, FaithintheWorkplace.com, http://www.christianitytoday.com/workplace/articles/interviews/davidmiller.html

Books

Frontline Christians in a Bottom-Line World, Linda Rios Brook (Destiny Image Publishers, 2005; ISBN 0768429668)

God at Work: The History and Promise of the Faith at Work Movement, David Miller (Oxford University Press, 2006; ISBN 0195314808)

Made to Count: Discovering What to do with Your Life, Bob Reccord and Randy Singer (Thomas Nelson, 2005; ISBN 0849908914)

Roaring Lambs, Robert Briner (Zondervan, 2000; ISBN 0310234190)

Notes

Is it possible to thrive at work and still have energy for a healthy family life?

Luke 10:38–42

SESSION 6

BALANCING ACT—HANDLING THE DEMANDS OF WORK AND HOME

■

Underneath the surface of many of our lives runs a current of stress. We feel pulled so many different directions—work, marriage, parenting, church, relationships—that we experience very little peace. Instead of living the way we desire, we let the demands of these various responsibilities gobble up our time and focus, leaving very little energy for God or our families.

Randy Frazee's fast-paced lifestyle and demanding job led to family problems and insomnia. Ramona Cramer Tucker was brought to tears by the pressures she felt by the demands placed on her. But both Frazee and Tucker have found freedom by striking a balance in life and setting some strict boundaries for themselves and their families. In this study, we'll look at their ideas in "Fried!" and "Just Say 'No!'" to generate discussion on how Christians can juggle the demands of work and home.

■ Before You Meet

Read "Fried!" by Ginger Kolbaba from *Marriage Partnership* magazine and "Just say 'No!'" by Ramona Cramer Tucker from *Today's Christian Woman* magazine.

FRIED!

Stress-related insomnia prompted Randy Frazee to set new boundaries to find the sunny side of life.

Interviewed by Ginger Kolbaba

Randy Frazee was fried. His demanding work schedule had taken such a toll on his marriage, family, and health that he suffered insomnia for forty-five days straight. Finally, he went to a physician who informed him that the insanity of his fast-paced life had caught up with him. He had three choices: move to Borneo; take medication, which would only temporarily relieve the symptoms; or radically change his lifestyle.

Randy opted for the last choice. Eight years later, his marriage and health have never been stronger. "I sleep like a baby now. And so does my wife!" he says.

In this *Marriage Partnership* interview, Randy, author of *Making Room for Life* (Zondervan), explains the secret to slowing down, enjoying life and love, and finding joy again.

You made a radical change to your lifestyle. What was it?

Randy: After my doctor's appointment, I began to study Genesis to see if God had anything to say about my situation. In Genesis 1, I noticed these statements: "And there was evening, and there was morning—the first day," and "And there was evening and morning—the second day." It does that for the entire creation account.

I realized that the Hebrews followed that account: at 6:00 p.m. they began their day ("and there was evening and morning"). Whatever was first was most important. So for them, the most important part of the day, the relational "season," began at sunset. No rushing, no work. Just a focus on their relationships with God and with others.

I discussed the lifestyle change with my wife, Rozanne, and then we told the kids. We set 6:00 p.m. as the definitive time to be done working for the day. That created a boundary that said we're going to have time for relationships. If something doesn't get finished, it can wait until the next day.

That shift must have been difficult to make.

It was! During the first few months I tapped my fingers on the dinner table and thought, *What am I supposed to do with all this time?*

What did you do?

We made the evening meal the first item on our agenda. We have dinner together as a family every night. In our family the meal is a festival. It's not considered a "to do" list for my wife. If there's one thing you want to do for your marriage, don't miss the evening meal. There's something about sharing a meal and conversation that's incredibly powerful.

Then Rozanne and I go for a walk, sit on the back porch and take in nature, or our family plays a board game or reads a good book together. The possibilities are endless.

But you mentioned no work. Doesn't making a meal and cleaning up constitute work?

We consider that an extension of the festival. Everyone jumps in to help: our kids set the table, cut the vegetables, someone else cooks. Afterward, we all clean up, do the dishes, and put everything away.

So even that becomes relational?

Yes! I know a couple who live this way. For years they didn't have a dishwasher. Recently, they purchased one, but not too long afterward returned it to the company. They found that washing and drying dishes was a great opportunity for conversation, and they missed that. So they said, "Come get it. We enjoy talking to each other during washing and drying dishes."

What do you talk about during dinner?

We simply ask, "Tell me about your day," and every person gets to share.

This is what life is all about—listening to the unfolding pages of the novel of the people God has put into your life.

So Rozanne gets a chance to say, "Let me tell you about my day. I got up . . ." And she walks through all the experiences of her day. At the end of the sharing we ask, "How would you rate your day on a scale of 1 to 10?"

When we first started, I'd say, "Don't rush. Tell me everything." And my wife and family would say, "I feel like I'm talking too much." I'd say, "Listen. This is what we've been waiting for all day. So just relax. We're not in any hurry."

I share my day last as the wrap up. And I have to be invited to share my day, just like everyone else.

You share even the mundane stuff?

Mundane is great. It's amazing how much you learn from mundane. You discover so much about a person in terms of how they share their day.

I think couples often underestimate the value of having your spouse look in your eyes and say, "I'm reading a lifetime novel here. I don't know how it ends, and I want to hear how it's all coming together." When you stream day in and day out together, you start learning things about a person that makes it a rich experience.

How has this lifestyle affected your marriage?

It's unbelievable! Before, I'd spend a little time in the evening with Rozanne, then I'd go back to work. Because I knew I was going back to work, I was often distracted in the time we *were* together.

Now that I don't go back to work in the evenings, I'm more relaxed, and we have a greater devotion to each other. We have the commitment to spend time together. We've never had that in our life before. But we do now because we created it.

It's changed our priorities. Six to 10:00 p.m. is our destination. When we give ourselves this, not only are we fulfilling what God intended for us, but we're also making our life balanced, we get better sleep, and get more work done during the day.

For most of our twenty-three years of marriage, I lived with the notion that my work was the most important thing and that relationships recharged my work. But in reality God didn't create relationships to recharge work; he created me for relationships. We were created *to* work but we were created *for* relationships. When I'm with my mate in the evening, I've arrived at my destination.

And romance?

Our intimacy level has soared! It's created a wonderful environment.

Romance is a process, not an event. And the meal conversation especially gives us an opportunity to begin the process. There's nothing like the sense of being heard and valued.

This lifestyle sounds so wonderful! But honestly, how realistic is this? Especially when some people don't even get home from work until six o'clock!

I'll be honest—it was a challenge when we first started. I'm this Type A, hard-driving person, so it was difficult to shut that off. I doubt I could have been talked into trying it had I not hit a crisis in my life.

God created us with a work cycle. We can work six days from 6:00 a.m. to 6:00 p.m. and take off one day. After 6:00 p.m. on those six days we need to enter into the relational season of the day and be replenished.

This is doable. But a couple has to sit down and make a list of the things they do on a routine basis—such as laundry, grocery shopping, or other house-related items. Then they need to ask, "When can we schedule these?" If a couple follows that schedule, they can actually have their evenings. Opt for doing things on Saturday that otherwise you'd do in the evening. Rozanne and I have a master list of things that need to be done, and we identify which ones are the priorities.

I know people would say that's rigid. The thing they don't understand is I'm not a rigid person. I've had to put myself under a stricter environment in order to create balance in my life and marriage.

For instance, I used to get up and work on the house with no boundaries, and it was oftentimes after dinner before I stopped. Now on Saturday mornings, I work three hours on house projects. That says working on the house is important but not extremely important. Everything has to be put in its place.

That seems as if you'd always be behind in your chores and workload, though.

There's a principle that says work takes all the time allotted to it. What we learned is that when you set a deadline for your work, you'll have a greater tendency to get more work done. Couples who don't create boundaries end up letting their work extend into all hours.

But what about kids with all their activities?

I believe kids' activities are a huge deterrent to making room for marriage. It's been ingrained into us that if we're going to be good parents we have to have our kids involved in everything.

My biggest problem with too many kids' activities is that they take us away from the one thing we're created for, the relational time of a shared meal. Prior to middle school, kids' sports are basically driven by volunteers. And volunteers have to wait until they get off work in order to run the practices or the game. And they have to do them before the sun goes down. That means they're doing practices during dinner.

So many couples we know go in two different directions because their kids are involved in evening activities. When they return to the house at ten o'clock after gulping down Taco Bell, stressed out, there's no way they're ready for romance or balance. They're worn out. And instead of connecting relationally with their spouse, they turn on the television.

How can couples incorporate this lifestyle?

Agree to the vision. They need to understand why they need to do this. Then learn how to get your work and chores done. Set a boundary. From six in the morning to six at night is the season for work. That's half of my life. When you say it that way it seems extremely reasonable that we could give half of our life to work and get the work done.

Rather than jumping into the lifestyle, which may be a shock to your family, try it for one day a week. See how successful that becomes. But stick to that boundary!

Or start by committing to share a meal where you talk about each other's day. Then maybe one evening instead of going back to work, take a walk together. If you don't go back to work you're going to find a whole different relationship.

How do you get both spouses on that same vision? Especially if a spouse says, "My time at six o'clock is my own. I've worked hard. I want to sit in front of the TV and veg."

One reason people watch TV is because they have no energy. When they come home, they're so fried that watching TV is a way of vegging out. When you live a balanced life, you've got energy in the evening. I know this from personal experience.

Now that we're living a balanced life, I can't tell you the last time I watched TV. Not because I'm against TV. I'm not.

I watched TV because I was fried. Now that I'm no longer fried, I just don't find it compelling.

So you haven't seen *Desperate Housewives*?

{Laughs} I used to live with one!

Look, even if you start with just one night a week, as a married couple you'll find that the change will enhance your romance, improve your sleep, lower your irritability, and give you a sense that you're finally making room for life. Ultimately most people I know think that one of these days they're going to make room for life. And for them that means sitting on a lawn chair, not being rushed, sipping tea. But to me, I'm not going to wait until I retire to make room for life and my marriage. I'm not going to wait until the bottom falls out. I'm not going to wait until all my activities and projects are done.

I'm going to stop. I'm going to start making room for life right now. And it's just as simple as creating this little relational/work boundary. I'm convinced if you try it once, it's going to be your favorite night of the week. And then that will give you the encouragement to do it twice.

Randy Frazee is a Teaching Pastor at Willow Creek Community Church and is the author of many books, including Making Room for Life.

Ginger Kolbaba is an author and the editor of Marriage Partnership *magazine, a sister publication of* Christianity Today.

("Fried!" was originally published in Marriage Partnership, *Fall 2005.)*

JUST SAY "NO"!

Why it might revolutionize your life.

by Ramona Cramer Tucker

My life hit the fan one ordinary weekend.

I was in the midst of running errands when it happened. I'd just settled into my car seat when I realized I'd forgotten the bills I intended to mail. As I dashed inside, the phone rang.

"Hey, Mona," my friend said cheerfully. "I haven't seen you in ages. Want to get together today?"

"Uh, sure, what time?" I said, distracted by my "to do" list. We set up the time and place, and I hung up the phone.

Then, on my way back to the car, I did something that startled even me: I sat down on the big rock by my driveway and cried so hard, I couldn't catch my breath.

Later that night, after my three-year-old was tucked into bed, I pondered why my friend's phone call had brought me to tears. My emotional meltdown showed me how stressed-out I was by life's demands—many of them self-induced. I needed to take better charge of my life. After all, God hadn't created me to run around constantly "chasing the wind" (Ecclesiastes 1:14)—which was exactly what I felt I was doing!

The answer to my problem narrowed down to a simple word: "No." But the problem was that "yes" rolled off my tongue so easily that "no" seemed cumbersome . . . even embarrassing. So if someone needed snacks for the office, I'd bring them. If my child's playgroup was meeting, I organized not only the activity, but the crafts too. Add all this to working full-time, or full-time-plus when a rush project came along, and it's no wonder I was exhausted. Eventually I taped a neon "Just Say NO!" sign to my phone. Once I'd said "no" a few times, my lips began to form the word more confidently. It's still not easy, but I'm gradually gaining more balance in my life.

Are *you* feeling exhausted? If so, you may need to say the word "no" more often, too. Here's how.

Know Yourself . . . and Your Slots

What's your energy level? Personality? Family situation? How much "regroup" time do you need? Do you crave interaction, or run from it?

Whether you're an introvert or an extrovert, trying to please everyone by "doing" only brings about exhaustion or bitterness. And that's certainly not the way God calls us to live. Psalm 139:1–3 makes it clear: "O Lord, you have searched me and you know me. You know when I sit and when I rise; you perceive my thoughts from afar. You discern my going out and my lying down; you are familiar with all my ways." God knows your personality intimately because he made you, and he doesn't expect you to be someone you're not. He also knows you need to stop sometimes and rest.

So figure out how many activities a week you're comfortable with, and then consider those "available slots." For instance, my friend Mary craves time alone since she works in a busy office. One evening out a week is enough for her, so that's all she schedules. On the other hand, Claudia, a friend with incredible energy, schedules four evenings out and still longs for another!

When I was single and worked full-time, I booked every lunch during the week. After all, it was a great opportunity to grow relationships with someone other than my roommate. But after a year of running every day from work to lunch with a friend and then back to work, I discovered I needed some downtime. So I made a personal policy to book only three lunches a week and to save the other two for "necessity runs" (to buy groceries or run to the post office), or simply for some me-time (even if it meant sitting alone in my car to read an encouraging psalm while I ate my sandwich). When I got married, I lunched with friends twice a week and set a standing weekly lunch date with my sister, since it was more difficult for us to get together after work. Our Wednesday lunch date continues to this day.

Instead of blindly booking activities simply because they arise, make sure you save the slots in your schedule you need for "sanity time."

Learn to Prioritize

Some of your stress-inducing situations may be nonnegotiable—such as traveling for your job or keeping up with an energetic toddler.

But other activities may be negotiable, such as hosting a wedding shower, chairing a "Fun Fair" at your school, or attending a Pampered Chef party. The crucial question is this: Do these negotiable activities stress you out . . . or energize you? Your answer will reveal whether or not your life is in balance. If your blood pressure rises when you even *think* about the activity, why not take a pass?

Recently I was invited to three product-demonstraton parties in friends' homes—all in one week. After thinking through my priorities (one of them being time for my husband in the evenings) and praying about my use of my time, I said "no" to all three.

Although I felt guilty turning down the invites, I also felt relieved when I hung up the phone after each of these conversations. And because I'd said "no," I had the time and energy to say "yes" to an impromptu stroll later in the week—complete with a picnic and a chat by a bubbling fountain—with my soul-rejuvenating friend Linda.

God alone knows what's ahead for us and can help us sort out our priorities. As Jeremiah 29:11–13 says, "For I know the plans I have for you . . . plans to prosper you and not to harm you, plans to give you hope and a future." But Scripture also says, "Commit your way to the Lord" (Psalm 37:5). We need to ask God to guide us—so we'll do what *he* has for us instead of doing everything that comes our way. Then we won't have to worry about "missing out."

Set a Limit—and Stick to It!

To most people, it's the getting together that counts, not the length of the stay. Even a short lunch can mean as much as an all-day outing. And telling friends or coworkers, "I have from 12:30 to 1:30 free for lunch. Would that work?" sets comfortable parameters for you.

Recently I had a Saturday with nothing planned—a rare treat indeed. I was looking forward to organizing my neglected photos when a good friend phoned to invite me to an impromptu party that was to start at 6 o'clock. But because my "to do" list at home had been growing, I said, "I'd love to come. But I won't be there until 9 o'clock because I have to get some things done at home first." This response allowed me to be a real friend—and also protected me from a too-scheduled weekend.

Many of us juggle multiple roles, including keeping up a house/apartment, working either inside or outside the home, and playing "relationship fix-it" for people we love. Add a boyfriend or husband, kids, or in-laws and it's no wonder we feel overwhelmed at times! But setting a time limit—then sticking to it—can work wonders in balancing the demands of your multifaceted life.

Be Proactive

I've discovered if I wait for others to come to me, I react by jumping to action and marking my calendar before I really have a chance to evaluate the activity or my looming schedule. Initiating activities gives me time for advance planning; it prepares me not only physically, but also emotionally.

So don't wait for others to contact you. Contact family and friends first. "I'd love to get together. How about two Saturdays from now, from 1:00–3:00?" When you do receive a phone call, say, "That sounds like fun. Let me check my schedule and get back to you." That will give you the emotional distance to evaluate your week realistically.

A friend of mine once quipped, "We women accomplish 90 percent of the world's workload . . . and we look and feel like it, too!" The reality is, we're afraid of letting people down even if we're driving ourselves crazy with activities. It's no surprise that "no" seems like a four-letter word we must avoid at all costs.

But "no" isn't a dirty word—in fact, sometimes it's one of the healthiest things we can say. After all, sometimes we have to say "no"—even to good things—in order to say "yes" to the *best* things. If we're constantly scurrying around like the well-known Martha in Luke 10:38–42, we won't have time to sit, like Mary, at Jesus's feet.

So go ahead . . . say "no" loudly. It won't kill you. In fact, it just may revolutionize your life.

Ramona Cramer Tucker, a regular contributor to Today's Christian Woman, *is Senior Editor for Tyndale House Publishers. She and her family live in the Chicago area. ("Just Say 'No'!" was originally published in* Today's Christian Woman, *September/October 2004.)*

Open Up

Select one of these activities to launch your discussion time.

Option 1

Discuss one of these icebreaker questions:

- If you could have one extra hour in the day, each day this week, what would you do with it? Why?

- When have you felt "fried"? Describe a time when trying to balance competing demands took a toll on your life.

Option 2

As a group, try at least two of these balance challenges:

- Walk across the room with a large book (such as a dictionary) balanced on your head. (No hands!)

- See how long you can balance a spinning basketball on your finger.

- Time how long you can balance on the tip-toes of one foot.

Afterward, talk about these questions:

- Which balance challenge was the toughest?

- How difficult is it for people to balance the demands of work and home? Share examples of people you know who seem to do it well or, alternately, people whose lives appear very out of balance.

■ The Issue

It's not uncommon to hear people engaged in a bragging contest about who is the busiest. We seem to wear it as a badge of honor that we never have a spare minute to think straight! Long hours at the office can leave people exhausted and without any emotional or physical energy to devote to relationships at home like marriage or parenting. For stay-at-home parents, the overlap between "work" and "home" can leave them feeling that their work is never done.

- Brainstorm together all the negative consequences of failing to strike a proper balance between work and home-life. How can this affect us personally (spiritually, physically, emotionally)? How does it affect our loved ones? How might it negatively affect our work?

■ Reflect

Take a moment to read Luke 10:38–42. Jot down a few notes and observations about this passage: How would you put the key ideas in your own words? What stands out to you most? What questions or issues does this passage raise for you?

Let's Explore

Our "home life" deserves our energy and focus.

- The demands of work can be relationally, intellectually, and physically exhausting. What are some of the stressors and demands placed upon you in your workplace?

Oftentimes, people want to "check out" at the end of a work day rather than invest energy in their spouse or children. Frazee comments on the tendency to check out in front of the TV, saying,

> One reason people watch TV is because they have no energy. When they come home, they're so fried that watching TV is a way of vegging out. When you live a balanced life, you've got energy in the evening. I know this from personal experience.
>
> Now that we're living a balanced life, I can't tell you the last time I watched TV. . . . I watched TV because I was fried. Now that I'm no longer fried, I just don't find it compelling.

- How do you usually feel at the end of a typical day of work? How do you wish you felt?

- Imagine an evening after work in which you didn't feel stressed or tired. What would you most want to do with your family? How would this compare to "vegging out"?

In his interview, Randy Frazee said:

> For most of our twenty-three years of marriage, I lived with the notion that my work was the most important thing and that relationships recharged my work. But in reality God didn't create relationships to recharge work; he created me for relationships. We were created *to* work but we were created *for* relationships. When I'm with my mate in the evening, I've arrived at my destination.

- What's your response to this idea? How might it change your daily work if you considered your relational time with family to be the "destination" of your day?

Say "no" to the good so you can say "yes" to the best.

Too often our schedules run away with us. There's *always* more work to do. And in addition to work are the demands of kids' activities, church involvement, time with friends, and so on. But instead of letting external factors overrun our lives and determine how we live, we can take control by zeroing in our focus onto the most important things in our lives.

In her article, Tucker says, "Sometimes we have to say 'no'—even to good things—in order to say 'yes' to the best things. If we're constantly scurrying around like the well-known Martha in Luke 10:38–42, we won't have time to sit, like Mary, at Jesus's feet." Read Luke 10:38–42.

- Was something wrong with what Martha was doing? After all, she was doing important work—and it needed to be done. Explain your thoughts.

- What "better thing" did Mary chose? What does it mean for us to choose "the better thing"?

- What are some of the "better things" in your life that God may want you to choose to focus on? How would it enrich your life to be able to put more energy and focus on these "better things"?

We can only find balance when we set both priorities and boundaries.

- Society promotes the idea that we can have it all—success at work in a high-powered career and a happy, healthy home-life. But is this idea really true in your experience? Explain.

Instead of aiming to "have it all," both Frazee and Tucker seem to suggest that we should focus our efforts on just a few specific priorities. Further, Jesus points out in Luke 10 that Mary made a *choice*. She could not have it all; she could not simultaneously busily work and sit at Jesus's feet. Zeroing in on a few priorities ultimately means choosing to give up other things—and this may involve some negative consequences. It may involve letting some commitments to church, hobbies, or friends go in order to have more time at home. It may mean letting housework slide a bit. It may involve working less hours and thus foregoing a possible promotion. It may even involve getting a less demanding job!

- When you think about your top priorities in life, what are the main hurdles that seem to get in the way of your focus on those priorities? What might you need to give up or sacrifice to better focus on your priorities?

Frazee comments, "I've had to put myself under a stricter environment in order to create balance in my life and marriage." Similarly, Tucker talks about priorities she set in order to have a more healthy pace in her life.

- Describe the priorities and boundaries discussed by both Frazee and Tucker. What stands out to you most about their ideas? Are these principles that might fit in your life? Why or why not?

Going Forward

In the Warrack Lectures of 1958 delivered in Scotland (and published under the title *The Preacher's Calling to Be a Servant*), D. T. Niles offered these words:

> Hurry means that we gather impressions but have no experiences, that we collect acquaintances but make no friends, that we attend meetings but experience no encounter. We must recover eternity if we are to find time, and eternity is what Jesus came to restore. For without it, there can be no charity.

And Frederick W. Faber wrote in the 1800s:

> There is hardly ever a complete silence in our soul. God is whispering to us well-nigh incessantly. Whenever the sounds of the world die out in the soul, or sink low, then we hear these whisperings of God. He is always whispering to us, only we do not always hear, because of the noise, hurry, and distraction which life causes as it rushes on.

- What stands out to you the most from these two quotes? How do they inspire, convict, or challenge you?

Break into pairs to discuss these final questions:

- In light of what you've discussed in this study, what needs to change in your pattern of thinking about the various demands placed on you at work and at home? How is God prompting you to change?

- Narrow your focus to one upcoming day this week. How will you alter your focus and your use of time to better balance your work with your family relationships? What will you do during your time with your family on that day?

Pray with your partner, asking God to give them the courage and strength to seek the "better thing" God has for them in life.

■ Want to Explore More?

Recommended Resources

Want to explore this topic further? Here are some resources that will help.

A Minute of Margin: Restoring Balance to Busy Lives, Richard A. Swenson M.D. (NavPress, 2003; ISBN 1576830683)

Balance That Works When Life Doesn't: Simple Steps to a Woman's Physical and Spiritual Health, Susie Larson (Harvest House Publishers, 2005; ISBN 0736916423)

Finding Balance from the Inside Out, Sheila Jones (Discipleship Publications, 2002; ISBN 1577821793)

Getting a Grip: Finding Balance in Your Daily Life, InterAction Series, Bill Hybels, Kevin Harney (Zondervan 2005; ISBN 031026605X)

It All Comes Out in the Wash: Sorting Through Priorities When Your Load is Out of Balance, Judi Braddy (Beacon Hill Press, 2006; ISBN 0834122596)

Making Room for Life—Trading Chaotic Lifestyles for Connected Relationships, Randy Frazee (Zondervan, 2004; ISBN 0310250161)

Meditations for Living in Balance, Anne Wilson Schaef (HarperCollins, 2000; ISBN 0062516434)

Motherhood in the Balance: Children, Career, Me, and God, Catherine Wallace (Morehouse Publishing, 2001; ISBN 081921873)

The Search for Balance, Jill Briscoe (Cook Communications, 2003; ISBN 0781439558)

Why is rest from work so important to God?

Genesis 2:1–3

Exodus 20:8–11

Psalm 23:1–4, 131:2

T.G.I.S.—THANK GOD IT'S THE SABBATH!

■

Sundays looked different years ago. They were the days people went to church, got together with family or friends, and kicked back and relaxed. But as time went on, Sundays started looking like every other day. They became days to catch up on work or to shop. It became business as usual. And for many, business as usual is, well, extremely *busy*. We never seem to take a rest from work and to-do lists.

In "The Gift of Rest," author Lynne M. Baab shares how her family observes the Sabbath. Having lived in Israel, her family practiced a day of rest and worship as the Israelis do. When her family moved back to the States, they made the decision to continue treating the day as one set apart: a day of replenishment. Baab's article challenges us to re-think the Sabbath and the place of rest in our work-weary lives.

Before You Meet

Read "The Gift of Rest" by Lynne M. Baab from *Today's Christian Woman* magazine.

THE GIFT OF REST

How to embrace the blessings of the Sabbath

by Lynne M. Baab

When I first started observing the Sabbath twenty-five years ago, it wasn't by choice. My husband and I lived in Tel Aviv, Israel, at the time, and everything in our neighborhood—stores, movie theaters, and restaurants—closed from sunset on Friday to sunset on Saturday. Even the buses stopped running for twenty-four hours. Since we didn't own a car, this greatly affected our lives.

At first we struggled to find activities for Friday evenings and Saturdays. But after a few months, we began to enjoy a day with few entertainment options. We read, we walked, we talked. My husband sometimes went bird-watching in the field near our apartment. I wrote long letters. We napped. Sometimes we prayed together leisurely. We simply slowed down. We rested in God's love and experienced his grace.

Our Sabbaths in Israel became God's gift to us individually, and enriched our life as a couple. Through Sabbath-keeping, we experienced the truth that God's love for us isn't based on what we *do*. We yearned to keep growing in our ability to receive that unconditional love once we returned to the U.S.

Back in the States, our family decided to continue observing the Sabbath on Sundays. Our first son had been born in Israel, and our second son was born soon after we returned home. As a young family, we read to our children, took long walks, and went to the zoo and the park after church.

As the years passed and our children grew up, our Sabbaths changed. But two things stayed constant: a slower pace and no work.

Slow Down

Never did a culture need the Sabbath as ours does today. It pressures us to be productive 24/7. Everything we do has to look good and accomplish something. Nothing encourages us to stop. But the word "Sabbath" literally means stop, pause, cease, desist.

One young woman recently told me, "I'd like our family to observe the Sabbath. I've been reading books about it, talking with my husband and kids, and we're going to start soon."

"Great," I replied. "Tell me about what you plan to do and not do on your Sabbath."

"I love the idea of starting on Saturday at sunset with a festive meal," she explained. "I'd like to have special food, blessings for the children, prayers and candles, like Jewish people do. Maybe we could sing some songs. Then the next day, after we go to church, I hope we can read some Bible stories and do some crafts to help the kids center the day around God."

"What do you plan to *stop* doing on the Sabbath?" I asked.

She looked at me blankly. Slowing down hadn't figured into her Sabbath observance. She was focused solely on adding new activities.

We can easily bring our culture's values into our attempts to observe a Sabbath. We so easily forget the core meaning of the Sabbath—stopping and resting—that we end up turning our observance of it into one more thing to achieve.

We certainly want to experience God's presence on the Sabbath, but we need to experiment with unforced ways to do it. "Simple" is a great word to describe the ideal activities for the Sabbath. As soon as we're working too hard to achieve anything on the Sabbath, we've violated the central idea of the day.

One Jewish tradition bans intercessory prayer on the Sabbath because it's viewed as too much work. In that tradition, appropriate Sabbath prayers are prayers of thankfulness. On the Sabbath, I spend time focusing on the beauty of the world God made and the good gifts he's given me in the previous week. I try to rest in thankfulness. While I don't try to be "hyper-spiritual" all day long, I've discovered a little thought discipline goes a long way toward giving me a day that's restful and rejuvenating.

Take the Day Off

In the Ten Commandments, the Israelites are commanded to keep the Sabbath day holy, or separate, from the other weekdays. The marker of that holiness is the absence of work. But the Old Testament doesn't give many specifics about what constitutes work. One of the few clear commands forbids lighting a fire (Exodus 35:3). This mandate assured that daughters, wives, and female servants wouldn't be expected to cook. All the food had to be cooked before the Sabbath began, and the dishes washed afterward. The Sabbath granted rest to everyone, even the women who labored the other six days of the week.

In our time, what's the equivalent of "lighting a fire"? What are those actions that send *us* into work mode?

When we first returned to the U.S. years ago, I was a part-time student and stay-at-home mom. For me, work consisted of studying, housework, and shopping. For my husband, work involved anything from his paid job as well as house repairs and lawn mowing. We simply didn't do any of those tasks on Sundays.

Today, turning on my computer, balancing the checkbook, weeding my garden, and cooking put me into work mode. I know some people find gardening and cooking relaxing; those women have a different list of work activities to avoid on the Sabbath.

One woman who works at a desk job finds her best Sabbath activities involve vigorous exercise outdoors. For many people, being outside on the Sabbath—walking, riding bikes, flying kites, sitting on a park bench—helps them feel closer to God. Sabbath time outside can be a time of reflection and prayer alone, a time of relaxed conversation with a friend, or an exuberant playtime with family members or friends.

Many people also benefit from some silent time on their Sabbath day. One single woman who works in a people-intensive job spends her Sabbath afternoon entirely alone. Then she often meets up with friends at the end of the day for a special meal.

One mom with young children prepares a "Sabbath box" of special activities for her children. During one hour on Sunday afternoon, her children know they're expected to play alone, enjoying the delights in the Sabbath box while their parents get some silent time.

Some of the "work" from which we need a rest is mental. A woman I know tries to avoid worry on the Sabbath. She considers herself a worrier and feels overwhelmed at the thought of trying not to worry every day. One day a week, however, feels manageable. A day free—or at least mostly free—from worry has been a great gift to her.

Similarly, as a person who's disliked my body for as long as I can remember, I attempt to keep my Sabbaths free from obsessing about the way I look. On the Sabbath I don't try on clothes and I don't read novels with slim, beautiful heroines. When I find myself thinking negative thoughts about myself, I try to set them aside for the day.

My husband and I have received many gifts from our commitment to honor the Sabbath: a day to spend with our children—and each other—without needing to get something done. A day free of multitasking. A day free of striving for perfection and productivity. A day to rest in God's goodness. Over the years, these gifts have continued to bless us and grant us glorious freedom in Christ.

Lynne M. Baab is an author who lives in Washington. She is the author of Sabbath Keeping: Finding Freedom in the Rhythms of Rest (InterVarsity). ("The Gift of Rest" originally appeared in Today's Christian Woman, *September/October 2005.)*

Open Up

Select one of these activities to launch your discussion time.

Option 1

Discuss one of these icebreaker questions:

- How well-rested are you right now? Answer using a scale of 1 to 10 (1 meaning "completely frazzled" and 10 meaning "fully rested").

- What do you typically like to do to rest or relax?

- Now dream big: Picture in your mind the most restful day you can imagine. What would you do throughout that day? Where would you be? Who would you be with?

Option 2

Prepare five pieces of paper ahead of time by writing one of the five senses at the top of each sheet: Sight, Sound, Taste, Smell, and Touch.

Sit in a circle and take a moment to quietly think about experiences that are restful or relaxing to you. Then pass out the five papers so they are spread out relatively evenly around the circle.

If you have a paper, begin by writing one thing on the paper that is restful or relaxing to you in that sensory category. For example, you might write "birds singing" (sound) or "a warm breeze" (touch). After you've written your idea, pass your paper to the person next to you so he or she can write an answer. Continue to write answers and pass the papers around the circle for five minutes.

Read aloud all that's written on each paper, then discuss:

- What's your reaction to this list of feelings and sensations? How does thinking about these restful experiences make you feel?

■ The Issue

People are tired. Everyone is rushing to get somewhere. Even when families go on vacation, it's a standing joke that when they return home they'll need a vacation to rest up! People spend hours dreaming about time off from work, yet so few of us actually experience true rest.

- Why do you think rest is such a low priority in our world?

In generations past, keeping the Sabbath was a high priority for Christians; often Sabbath-keeping involved a strict set of rules for behavior that was not allowed (such as shopping or mowing the lawn) as well as expectations of what the day should involve (such as attending church—sometimes twice, eating a large Sunday meal, and dressing up). Only a few decades ago, most businesses in America (including grocery stores and restaurants) closed down on Sundays in observance of the Sabbath. For many American Christians today, though, the actual practice of Sabbath-keeping has faded from view as Sunday has become a day much like any other.

- Do you think the relaxed attitudes toward the Sabbath among many Christians today is a good thing or a bad thing? Explain.

Reflect

Take a moment to read Genesis 2:1–3; Exodus 20:8–11; and Psalm 23:1–4, 131:2 on your own, making notes about observations. What common themes and ideas stand out to you? In what ways do these teachings relate to the article you read? What questions do these passages raise for you?

Let's Explore

Rest is God's idea.

From the beginning of time, rest was God's idea. Read Genesis 2:1–3. God rested when he finished his work, giving us a pattern to follow. Even the seasons allow time for the earth to be replenished. Rest is God's idea.

- The Bible tells us God is all-powerful. So why do you think he rested on the seventh day?

Read Exodus 2:8–11.

- How does this passage make you feel? Guilty? Convicted? Resistant? Inspired? Hopeful? Explain.

- If God thinks resting on the Sabbath is a good idea, why do you think so many Christians ignore this?

- Do you think it matters if the day of rest is on Sunday? Why or why not?

Our bodies need to slow down.

Our bodies are wonderfully designed. Yet because we live in a fallen world, our bodies get tired, weak, and sometimes sick. To make sure we are in optimal health, we need to eat right, drink plenty of water, exercise, and have times of rest. A body that is constantly on the go needs time to replenish.

Jesus took care of his physical and emotional needs. His ministry was taxing; people everywhere needed him. Yet he knew when he needed to get off by himself. Luke 5:16 records that as his popularity grew, Jesus "often slipped away to be alone so he could pray." Often people share how much they have to do and how few hours of sleep they have gotten as if it is something to brag about. In contrast, our Savior took care of his body and his soul. When he needed rest, he got rest.

- Share about a time when many responsibilities prevented you from getting proper rest. How did it affect you physically, socially, and spiritually?

Read Psalm 131:2.

- Put this passage into your own words. What do you think the Psalmist means? Why do we need to take time to still and quiet our souls? What effect can that have on our minds and bodies?

- One of the fruits of the Spirit is peace (Galatians 5:22–23); do you think it's possible to have peace without having time to rest? Explain your answer.

In her article, Lynne Baab points out some of the things her family did as they rested on the Sabbath: "We read, we walked, we talked. My husband sometimes went bird-watching in the field near our apartment. I wrote long letters. We napped. Sometimes we prayed together leisurely. We simply slowed down. We rested in God's love and experienced his grace."

Many other cultures close shop, even on weekdays, for a short rest. On Sundays in these cultures, it is common to see groups of people leisurely walking, taking in the beautiful surroundings. Outdoor cafés are often filled with people just sitting and enjoying each other's company, a slower pace. As American Christians, we need to challenge our society's frantic pace so that our bodies and souls can be refreshed.

- Out of all the Sabbath-keeping practices Baab mentions in her article, which most appealed to you? Why? What other ideas do you have?

Finding time to rest is a challenge, but it's worth the effort.

For some, there may not be the luxury of a whole day to rest. Homes with one parent barely have enough hours in a day to get everything done before the coming week. But this is an important time for building relationships, spending time together, and resting. It's important to *make* time to rest, even when it seems like a challenge. The benefits are readily experienced, and after a while of planning to set that time aside, you'll get used to it and begin to schedule your week differently in order to keep that time sacred.

- What are some of the biggest challenges you face concerning getting enough rest?

Read Psalm 23:1–4. God actually *makes* us lie down in green pastures. When we study about sheep, we learn that they are not the smartest of creatures. They actually have to be forced to lie down. Our God cares for us as the sheep in his pasture. Lovingly he leads us to the greenest grass. With rod and staff he guides us in the paths he wants us to take, and when we need rest, he makes us lie down.

- What do the images of rest in this passage communicate to you about God's love and care for you?

- How does this inform your understanding of the Sabbath and God's purposes for it in your life? In practical terms, what experiences, habits, or activities help you to experience this "green-pastures" type of rest?

■ Going Forward

Baab says "the word 'Sabbath' literally means stop, pause, cease, desist." She tells of a time when she spoke with a woman who was inspired to practice the Sabbath in a meaningful way with lots of extra activities. Baab asked the woman, "What do you plan to *stop* doing on the Sabbath?"

- What is God calling you to "stop doing" on the Sabbath?

- In what ways could you distinguish between your Sabbath time (as a time that is holy and for the Lord) and other "chill out" time (that is focused on self, entertainment, and so on)?

Form pairs and talk with your partner about the goals and ideas this study has brought to mind for you as you consider Sabbath-keeping in your own life. Discuss these questions together:

- When you look back on all we've discussed, what do you see as your biggest obstacle to putting something like this into practice?

- What precautions might you need to take to ensure others will respect your commitment to rest?

Conclude your study by praying Psalm 23:1–4 together as a group.

■ Want to Explore More?

Recommended Resources

Want to explore this topic further? Here are some resources that will help.

Catch Your Breath: God's Invitation to Sabbath Rest, Don Postema (Faith Alive Christian Resources, 1997; ISBN 1562122398)

Celebrating the Sabbath: Find Rest in a Restless World, Bruce A. Ray (P. & R. Publishing, 2000; ISBN 0875523941)

Living the Sabbath: Discovering the Rhythms of Rest and Delight, Norman Wirsba (Baker, 2006; ISBN 1587431653)

Receiving the Day: Christian Practices for Opening the Gift of Time, Dorothy Bass (Jossey-Bass, 2001; ISBN 0787956473)

The Rest of God: Restoring Your Soul by Restoring the Sabbath, Mark Buchanan (Thomas Nelson, 2006; ISBN 0849918480)

Sabbath Keeping: Finding Freedom in the Rhythms of Rest, Lynne M. Baab (Inter-varsity Press, 2005; ISBN 0830832580)

Sabbath Sense: A Spiritual Antidote for the Overworked, Donna Schaper (Augsburg/Fortress, 2004; ISBN 0806690178)

Sabbath Time, Tilden H. Edwards (Upper Room, 2003; ISBN 0835898628)

Sabbath: Finding Rest, Renewal, and Delight in Our Busy Lives, Wayne Muller (Bantam 2000; ISBN 0553380117)

The Sabbath: Entering God's Rest, Barry Rubin and Steffi Rubin (Messianic Jewish Publishers, 2003; ISBN 188022674X)

Is retirement the end of one's career . . . or the beginning of a new one?

Matthew 6:19–21

Galatians 5:13

Ephesians 5:15–16

SESSION 8

RETIREMENT—FINISHING WELL

■

Just hearing the word *retirement* conjures images of playing golf, going on a cruise, or playing with grandchildren. While leisurely pursuits bring a certain amount of satisfaction, many retirees are finding they want more—to spend their latter years in significant service to a cause greater than their personal pleasure. Most people want their lives to matter as they look down their final path.

Decisions about retirement should be made before you settle into a routine that becomes too comfortable to change. Why choose a deliberate path of service in retirement? How does God want you to use your talents and life experience? How do you find significance in the kind of work that God would have you do? These are the questions we'll be discussing in this study based on a *Christianity Today* article by Christine J. Gardner.

Before You Meet

Read "Finishing Well" by Christine J. Gardner from *Christianity Today* magazine.

FINISHING WELL

After achieving success, early retirees are finding significance in second-career mission assignments.

by Christine J. Gardner

Nelson Malwitz was having a midlife crisis. At fifty, he was at the top of his game. As corporate director of chemical research for Sealed Air Corporation in Danbury, Connecticut, the company that invented Bubble Wrap, Malwitz achieved seven patents for plastic foam technology. He served as an adult Sunday-school teacher at Walnut Hill Community Church, a congregation he helped found. He had a wife, Marge, and two teenage sons, Jonathan and David, who loved him. But something was missing. Then he remembered Urbana.

The year was 1967. Raised in the Christian and Missionary Alliance denomination, Malwitz was twenty-one when he attended the InterVarsity student missions conference in Urbana, Illinois. Reflecting the idealism of the time, Malwitz wanted to change the world, so he committed his life to missions. But family, career, and mortgage payments soon got in the way.

Now with a view from middle age, Malwitz decided to revisit his dream and pursue a second career in missions. But he quickly found missions agencies were unprepared for a skilled professional in his fifties. "It was so difficult to get in, and I had no idea where the point of entry was," Malwitz says.

Gene Shackelford, a friend from church, had a similar experience. At fifty-nine, he retired as a vice president of Union Carbide. He and his wife were active in Bible Study Fellowship and participated on his congregation's missions committee, but it took them three years to find a position in missions. "I thought, *That's way too long*," Malwitz says.

"The task is way too difficult for people to get a significant second career if the missions infrastructure is not ready to take people." So Malwitz decided his contribution to missions would be to encourage others from his generation to consider second careers in missions and to help them through what he calls "the missions minefield."

Malwitz founded Finishers Project in 1996. "As you hit fifty, you no longer count your years from the time you were born, but you count the amount of time you have left," he says. "The big idea has to do with finishing well." Like Malwitz, who calls himself "the generic evangelical baby boomer sitting in the pew," millions of boomers, identified as those born between 1946 and 1965, are approaching retirement with their nests empty and their 401(k)s full. In 2001, the leading edge of the 82 million-strong group turned fifty-five, for an estimated total of 21 million boomers fifty years or older. Malwitz has determined that 4.6 million of them are evangelicals. If 1 percent is interested in missions, 46,000 individuals could be available for ministry.

They are the healthiest, wealthiest, and best-educated retirees ever. These evangelical boomer "finishers" (or "second-halfers") may want to start second careers in missions. They have already achieved success in their careers; now they want to achieve significance. Their idealism—as well as their skills and money—could help revive flagging North American missions.

Search for Significance

Michael Darby, a senior vice president at Shearson Lehman, had been a stockbroker for thirty years, and his wife, Elizabeth, had owned a retail store for thirteen years when they started feeling burned out. "We didn't have the joy of going to work like we used to," Michael says.

A teaching cassette by television preacher Charles Stanley about discovering God's will and a job offer from a friend at Focus on the Family prompted the Darbys to consider career opportunities in ministry. A visit with friend Bruce Wilkinson at Walk Thru the Bible confirmed their call to missions.

But panic quickly set in. They had a business to liquidate, a house to sell, and a career to conclude—but at least their children were grown and they had no financial debt. The Darbys decided to let God take care of the details. "If it's his calling, we're not supposed to worry about those things," Michael says. "We're just supposed to obey."

In 1991, Michael retired early at fifty-four and Elizabeth, then forty-nine, sold her store so they could work with CoMission, a cooperative effort by eighty organizations to teach Christian values in Russian public schools. After short trips to the country, the Darbys joined a team from Navigators to live in Rostov, Russia, for a year to disciple new believers. The Darbys exchanged a home on the Florida coast for university housing with no hot water, infrequent heat and electricity, and a view of a garbage dump; but they considered themselves blessed to have rediscovered God's purpose. Now living in Georgia, the Darbys are working with Navigators on a new program to help other finishers determine their giftedness.

Ken and Pat Kingston assumed they would retire one day and move to Florida or Arizona. But retirement came sooner than they expected when Ken, a middle-school teacher in Crystal Lake, Illinois, for twenty-nine years, had an early retirement option at age fifty-nine. In 1991, they seized the opportunity to pursue a lifelong dream of becoming missionaries with Wycliffe Bible Translators.

The Kingstons believe God orchestrated the timing. Pat's mother, who had been living with the Kingstons, had died a month earlier. Their youngest son married the previous summer.

But credit card debt concerned them, along with leaving their four grandchildren, all of whom lived within two blocks of their home. Ken's pension helped, but the Kingstons still had to raise support.

The Kingstons "adopted" many new grandchildren in Lima, Peru, where Ken used his experience as an educator to start a school for missionary children while Pat served in the Wycliffe office. After six years, the Kingstons returned home for a year, but they now are packing for a three-year assignment in Kenya. "[Retired] people are traipsing around the country in RVs," laughs Pat. "I think that would be the most boring life I could ever imagine."

Both the Darbys and the Kingstons achieved success in their careers, but they wanted something more. Bob Buford would say they sought significance. Buford, whose book *Halftime* (Zondervan, 1994) is the unofficial guidebook for finishers, says that for retirees who choose service over leisure, "the payoff is blessedness."

A recent survey of six hundred evangelical boomers, sponsored by Finishers Project, indicates 61 percent would like to retire early and pursue a second career. Fifty-four percent say they would consider a second career in missions. Eighty-one percent want to be able to serve with their spouse. "They want to leave a legacy," says Rod Beidler, director of international recruitment for Navigators.

Missions Dilemma

As early retirees search for significance in the second half of their lives, some missions leaders are wondering whether self-absorbed boomers are willing to make the costly sacrifices necessary to serve in overseas ministry. But with the leveling off of church commitment to foreign missions, agency leaders may have few alternatives to draw in a significant number of fresh missions candidates.

The *Mission Handbook* (MARC, 1997) indicates that by 2000, more than 1 billion people still will not have heard the gospel message. Yet as the world's population increases, North American mission efforts have not.

"Basically, we've plateaued," says Jim Reapsome, founder of *Evangelical Missions Quarterly*, commenting on the current numbers of full-time North American missionaries. By contrast, the number of short-term missionaries—on assignments as short as two weeks—continues to rise.

There are more available missions positions than qualified candidates to fill them. TEAM is recruiting for seven hundred positions. Wycliffe has fifteen hundred openings. Servant Opportunity Network, a computer matching service for retirees, lists more than six thousand available jobs with more than two hundred missions agencies.

Ralph Winter, general director of Frontier Mission Fellowship, estimates non-Western missionaries will outnumber Western missionaries in the next few years. Missions experts point to the new ranks of cross-cultural missionaries from developing-world congregations as the result of centuries of missionary commitment from the Western church.

But in North America, the church's financial support of missions is steadily declining. According to *Money Matters: Personal Giving in American Churches* (Westminster John Knox Press, 1996), 10 to 15 percent of Protestant church budgets goes to foreign missions, roughly half the amount of what it was in the 1950s. *The State of Church Giving Through 1992* (empty tomb, inc., 1994) estimates that Protestant church members each gave only $20 to foreign missions in 1991, compared to $164 spent on soft drinks and $103 for sporting goods.

"[The church] is losing its zeal," says Larry Walker, southwest regional director for ACMC, which assists its one thousand member churches with their missions programs. "The older generation understood missions more." He says pluralism and materialism have changed the missions climate.

Christina Accornero, a board member of InterServe and Finishers Project, believes the church needs a missions revival. "We're going through a crisis in missions," she says. "Especially Americans, we're pretty comfortable with our things. There are many missionaries coming home on furlough who don't want to go back." Finishers Project could be the catalyst for revival. "I think it's a test—a God-directed test—to see if we are open to a new movement of the Spirit," Accornero says.

Overcoming Obstacles

Missions agency leaders agree that they need to update their processes to accommodate boomers. Malwitz, as a test to see how agencies would respond to a finisher, forwarded the name of Indiana financial consultant David Ober to two dozen missions agencies. Sixteen of the agencies made no effort to contact Ober. Eight sent standard information packets—data geared to recent college graduates, not older professionals with concerns about health insurance and financial planning.

Navigators' Rod Beidler says that when he started receiving calls from finishers looking for second careers, "we didn't know what to do with them. We were caught very much by surprise."

Ed Lewis, a recruiter with International Teams, says finishers know the primary need to spread the gospel worldwide. "They are up to the challenge and want to get involved," he says. "We don't want to put unnecessary obstacles in their path. And I think maybe, right now, we're doing that."

Mike and Linda Green, of Jupiter, Florida, shared a desire to use their skills in communications technology to further world evangelism. In 1994, Mike retired early at fifty-eight from a thirty-year career as a nuclear engineer and started his own business as a software consultant. Linda, then forty-nine, worked as an editor of an online financial publication. Their passion for missions had been fueled by Urbana, which Mike first attended in 1957 and they both attended in 1996. But the missions agencies they approached would not accept them because they both had earlier been divorced—twice for Linda and once for Mike, while he was a Christian.

Mike and Linda applied at six agencies, all of which turned them down. Most agencies terminated their applications early in the process. "Some just come right out and say, 'Sorry, we can't have divorced people as part of our organization,'" says Mike. One agency said they "had to limit their damages, so to speak," he says. The Greens' worst experience involved a missions agency that accepted them after numerous interviews, but later retracted their offer after a staff member threatened to leave if the organization hired a divorced couple. "It was painful at times," Mike says.

Culture Clash

Both boomers and missions agencies are anticipating a clash of cultures. The attributes of boomers that make them so appealing—spiritual and emotional maturity, professional skills, and financial security—may also create problems that could hinder missions objectives.

The largest cross-cultural adjustment a boomer may have to make is between the corporate and nonprofit worlds, especially if the boomer has left a leadership position. "If a finisher is a high-powered CEO-type, he's not going to be prepared to sweep the halls," says Winter.

Some finishers may expect a leadership position in missions, Lewis says, but it will take time for them to gain credibility with career missionaries who may feel threatened by finishers who seem to use missions as a hobby. He believes more finishers such as Michael Darby—who had no qualms about leaving a management position in finance to work as part of a discipleship team in Russia—are looking for a respite from the responsibilities of leadership.

Others, such as the Kingstons and the Greens, may want to use their professional skills in missions, but it may mean they will have to serve in a support role. If they are not wealthy enough to support themselves on retirement income alone, they may have a difficult time raising support. "We view missionaries as people going into hardship posts, maybe wrestling with cockroaches," says Art McCleary, a finisher who left a career in human resources to work for Senior Ambassadors for Christ. "But when they are in an office setting in the West, it is difficult to see them as missionaries."

Mike and Linda Green finally found computer positions with the Caleb Project in Littleton, Colorado, but they recently had to withdraw their acceptance because they could not raise enough support. After fifteen months of raising funds, the Greens had only 15 percent of their combined first-year support. By contrast, Mike's oldest daughter and her husband, who are leaving to plant a church with a Mennonite missions team in Albania, have raised their full support. Mike and Linda Green sold their house in August in anticipation of their move to Colorado. "We're back at square one in many ways," says Mike.

Another potential area of frustration is recruitment and training. Finishers say the hiring process is too slow, taking several months to several years before a candidate is accepted, trained, and has raised support.

In most cases, finishers are mature in their faith but have not had the formal Bible training required by most agencies. TEAM, for example, requires thirty semester hours of Bible classes for its full-time missionaries. Finishers Project is looking to develop a "Bible SAT" to accommodate those who are biblically literate but may not have the college transcripts to prove it.

The lack of a foreign language could also hinder a finisher's effectiveness in missions by limiting options to support roles in the United States or reliance on an interpreter.

But altering the training requirements to meet the needs of boomers is an area of serious concern for Winter, who sees a growing "amateurization" in missions. "I don't care if you have a PhD in marketing, [a finisher] still needs to know what missions is," he says. Otherwise, they will just be "sand in the machinery."

Drive-By Missions?

Despite the eagerness of missions agencies to retool their processes to attract finishers, some missions experts are skeptical. They fear finishers could change the focus of missions by demanding short-term options, disregarding indigenous leadership, and posing a threat to career missionaries.

Winter believes finishers will not want to spend their last years of life overseas, instead choosing "drive-by missions projects."

"For the most part, short-termers have given up trying to make a contribution to missions," Winter says. "It's kind of an expensive education, and almost a futile way of conducting missions."

But short-term missions opportunities could help finishers verify their commitment to longer-term assignments, says Paul McKaughan, president of the Evangelical Foreign Missions Association.

Missions experts herald the growth of indigenous leadership in missions and express concern over whether a new corps of Western finishers may be counterproductive to internationalization. "The role we played in the past is not the role we will play in the future," says McKaughan. "We will not be calling the shots from the West."

Ruth Tucker, visiting professor of mission at Trinity Evangelical Divinity School, says, "Our fix-it-upper mentality—that *we* can do it—it's passe." Finishers Project is "wrong-headed," she says, if nationals are not consulted first.

Bill O'Brien, director of the Global Center at Samford University, says finishers need to know the church in the Two-Thirds World is prospering, with an estimated one thousand sending agencies and more than forty thousand missionaries. North American Christians still have a pivotal role to play in missions—especially in the training of national leaders—but O'Brien says finishers need to understand they are the students in this process.

The agencies' eagerness to court finishers could be perceived as a slap in the face to career missionaries who bypassed opportunities for profitable careers. "Oftentimes, missionaries are a little bit offended by the fact that these people come in and 'haven't paid their dues,'" acknowledges Malwitz. "However, they're just going to have to get over it."

Historic Opportunity

Despite the concerns, Finishers Project is taking advantage of a historic opportunity. Plans are under way for an adult educational video, a toll-free number with information on job availabilities, and a finishers magazine. The idea is spreading around the globe: Malwitz has received calls from boomers in Canada, Germany, Ireland, New Zealand, South Africa, and Taiwan who want to start their own Finishers Project.

Thousands of boomers are approaching retirement and want a second chance to make a difference in their world; but a problem could arise if significance, not service, becomes their goal.

O'Brien warns that boomers' desire to become finishers should have more to do with meeting missions goals than their personal goals. Missions is "not just a flash-in-the-pan that gave me a warm, bubbly feeling because I felt significant for a minute," he says.

North American missions need the energy that comes from a new corps of impassioned missionaries. Finishers need to find significance in their retirement years. But finishers must move from the pursuit of personal fulfillment to fulfillment of the Great Commission—sharing the gospel with a world desperate to hear—if they want to use their life skills to nurture a young, but growing, church.

Christine J. Gardner recently finished her PhD at Northwestern University, and is now an assistant professor in the communications department at Wheaton College. ("Finishing Well" was originally published in Christianity Today, *October 5, 1998.)*

■ Open Up

Select one of these activities to launch your discussion time.

Option 1

Discuss one of these icebreaker questions:

- Imagine a new law was passed that required every able-bodied person to continue working until they were physically or mentally unable to do so, regardless of age. Would you continue doing what you did in your career, or would you change the type of work you perform? Explain.

- How would you describe your parents' or grandparents' views of retirement? What activities or rewards are/were associated with their post-work years?

- Describe the images that routinely come to mind when you think of your own retirement. How do you envision it? What are your main goals for retirement?

Option 2

Write each of your names on a slip of paper, then mix up the slips and redistribute them so that everyone has drawn the name of someone else in the group.

Take a paper and pencil and quickly sketch a cartoon that depicts how you imagine the person whose name you drew might spend his or her retirement years. Your sketch can be fun, funny, or serious—and it doesn't have to be a work of art! Do your best to depict that person *without* writing his or her name on the paper.

When everyone has had just a minute or two to create your sketches, one-at-a-time display your sketch and let the rest of the group guess who you portrayed.

Afterward, discuss:

- How well did the drawing of you match up with what you envision for yourself in retirement?

■ The Issue

If you haven't already heard, 77 million baby boomers are on track to become senior citizens in the next two decades. That means that approximately one quarter of the people in the U.S. will be of retirement age—when they can stop working if they choose, collect social security, qualify for Medicare benefits, and get senior citizens' discounts at just about every chain restaurant in the country. While these perks are helpful, increasing numbers of people are eagerly looking forward to retirement for completely different reasons. Some are even hoping they get downsized from their current jobs to free them up to take early retirement and get on with what they would prefer to be doing with their time: helping others.

Benevolence has taken on new meaning in recent years. Terrorist attacks, earthquakes, hurricanes, tsunamis, and the regular crises in our own churches and communities have created immense needs. But as people have responded with their time, energy, and money, they've gotten a taste of what it's like to truly make a difference in peoples' lives. Those who get involved are usually hooked because of the contentment service brings. Many want to do more for those in need, and retirement is seen as a wonderful opportunity to do this work.

Then there are those who aren't sure they can or should try to find a second career at their age. They are uncertain what they would do or how they would go about doing it. But both groups want to spend their later years doing something significant; to look back on their lives and feel that their choices about how to spend their retirement were good ones.

- How would you explain the dominant message about retirement coming from the larger culture? Why do you think it gets framed this way? What are the main forces that shape this message?

■ Reflect

Take a moment to read Matthew 6:19–21; Galatians 5:13; and Ephesians 5:15–16 on your own. Jot down a few notes and observations about the passages: What appear to be the key ideas in each passage? What inspires you or challenges you in these passages? What questions do these passages raise?

■ Let's Explore

Personal pleasure has its limits.

- For many, retirement is viewed as the reward for a lifetime of hard work; there's a sense that in retirement people are entitled to focus on themselves and take time to enjoy life. Is there truth in this idea? In what ways does Christian teaching support this idea and in what ways does it contradict it?

Ask the average person what comes to mind when they think of retirement and most will frame their answer in financial terms—for good reason. As more companies stop funding pensions, rumors about the demise of social security swirl, and healthcare costs take an ever bigger bite out of most people's paycheck, people are afraid of getting to retirement age and not having enough assets to live out the rest of their lives. In other words, we feel insecure about the future. This insecurity causes us to spend an inordinate amount of our time and energy accumulating and consuming goods for our own pleasure and security.

- Do you feel you have saved or will save enough financial assets to carry you through retirement and old age? Why or why not? Do you generally feel "secure" or "insecure" about your own retirement planning?

Read Matthew 6:19–21.

- Give some examples of both kinds of treasure Jesus referred to in Matthew 6: those we should store up and those we shouldn't. In practical terms, what does this mean in our daily lives?

Jesus's words cause us to pause and examine our motives for "storing up for ourselves." Although we need material goods to live, we are called to look beyond what we need to ensure that our heart is in the right place. "Your heart will be where your treasure is." In other words, the common notion that retirement is primarily a time to pull back and pursue personal pleasure is misplaced. Gardner notes how many retirees "have already achieved success in their careers; now they want to achieve significance." Retirement is a time for engagement, and pleasure can be replaced with contentment if our time and energy are well spent.

- What's the difference between success and significance? What constitutes a significant life when compared to a life poorly spent? Give examples.

- What role models can you think of that have lived a life of significance? What inspires or motivates you in their example? What have they taught you about the process of growing old?

Engaging in the work God has for you creates purpose and significance.

Contrary to popular views on retirement, we are not called out of the world in the later years of life. We find our true identity as God's people *in* the world that God made. We never "retire" from God's purpose and calling in our lives.

Read Galatians 5:13–14 and Ephesians 5:15–16.

- How would you sum up the main points of these passages in your own words? What stands out to you the most?

- How do these ideas compare or contrast with the way retirement is viewed in our culture?

Too often retirees voluntarily step out of the mainstream of life, marginalizing themselves, instead of staying squarely in it and seeing that they have much to contribute. The exercise of your gifts, talents, and skills in service to others is not only personally gratifying but also helps to build up the body of believers (see Romans 12:4–8). By virtue of more life experience, older adults typically have a wealth of experience to share.

Some will choose to fulfill their calling in the sphere God has them in right now. Others may choose a more radical alternative. Many retirees are finding their later life work in missions. Gardner cites a survey of six hundred evangelical boomers, sponsored by Finishers Project, which showed that 61 percent would like to retire early and pursue a second career. Fifty-four percent say they would consider a second career in missions.

The real question when it comes to retirement is not, "*Should* I be using my retirement to serve others?" but, "How can I faithfully pursue the work God has for me to do?"

- As you think ahead to retirement, identify at least one talent or skill you have that you would like to pass on to others. How could others potentially benefit from this? In what ways could this build up the body of believers in your church?

- As you plan for the future, have you ever considered using your retirement as a second career in missions? What does or doesn't appeal to you about this option? What are some other avenues of service in retirement that interest you?

■ Going Forward

Break into pairs to discuss these questions:

- How has this discussion influenced your perspective on retirement? How do you feel God may be speaking to you about this issue?

- In light of all you've discussed, consider this question: If you could construct your own retirement with no restrictions on money, time, or location, what would it look like? Why would you choose to do this?

Gather back together as a group and read this quote:

"As you hit fifty, you no longer count your years from the time you were born, but you count the amount of time you have left. The big idea has to do with finishing well."—Nelson Malwitz, founder of Finishers Project.

- Ultimately, what does it mean to you to "finish well"?

Pray together as a group, offering your dreams and plans for retirement to God and inviting God to replace them with *his* purposes for your retirement years. As you pray, hold your hands out with palms up as a physical representation of your surrender to God's will and your openness to his direction.

■ Want to Explore More?

Recommended Resources

Want to explore this topic further? Here are some resources that will help

Books

Don't Retire, REWIRE!, Jeri Sedlar and Rick Miners (Alpha Books, 2002; ISBN: 0028642287)

Half Time, Bob Buford (Zondervan, 1997; ISBN: 0310215323)

Live Your Calling, Kevin and Kay Marie Brennfleck (Jossey-Bass, 2004; ISBN: 0787968951)

Too Young to Retire: 101 Ways to Start the Rest of Your Life, Marika Stone, Howard Stone (Plume Books, 2004; ISBN: 0452285577)

Women Confronting Retirement: A Nontraditional Guide, Nan Bauer Maglin, Alice Radosh (Rutgers University Press, 2003; ISBN: 0813531268)

Organizations

The Finishers Project, http://www.finishers.org. The Finishers Project provides Christian adults information, challenge and pathways for discovery and processing of opportunities in ministry and missions—short-term or as a second career.

Bonus Small-Group Builder

from www.SmallGroups.com

You can find more helpful insights for small group health at **www.SmallGroups.com**.

THE WORKPLACE SMALL GROUP MOVEMENT

A Conversation with Stephen R. Graves

Steve Graves along with Tom Addington co-founded Cornerstone Group, Wellspring Partners and The Life@Work Co. These organizations are committed to providing leadership to people integrating faith and work by exploring ideas, connecting people, and using biblical principles to help organizations grow through biblical wisdom and marketplace excellence. Steve and Tom have authored many books including most recently Behind the Bottom Line *and* Clout, *both published by Jossey-Bass. Steve spoke to SmallGroups.com director Dan Lentz about developing small Christian communities in the workplace.*

SmallGroups.com: From your experience or research, how widespread are the occurrence of intentional Christian small groups that meet in the context of the workplace?

Steve: We have seen great interest and participation in workplace small groups. In fact, there is a hockey stick curve reflecting the need for information about creating Christian community in the workplace. Today, people in the workplace are personally engaged in realizing their most basic needs: information, inspiration, and community. These three elements are core to what everyone needs and searches for. More and more I see people being open to faith-based solutions to these needs. I see it everywhere. So much so, that I am willing to label the integration of faith-based community in the marketplace a serious God-movement that is going on right now. I believe there are five signs of a spiritual movement. One of the signs is that spiritual entrepreneurship begins to run rampant. There are so many "pop-corn" initiatives of spiritual entrepreneurship happening all over the country. We have seen this through countless clusters of folks who are getting together to talk about matters of faith over lunch, or on work-breaks. As we travel around the U.S. we have been amazed at the number of small group gatherings popping up everywhere. Sometimes it is church or para-church sponsored gatherings, or sometimes it is just a few people who sense a prompting to be intentional about offering Christian community to co-workers.

SmallGroups.com: Who is most likely to attend a workplace small group, already committed Christians . . . nominal Christians . . . or non-believers?

Steve: All of the above—depends on the sponsor group/person and their approach. Some that are attracting only committed Christians are more of a roll-over Sunday school class that happens to meet outside the church building, but many workplace small groups are outreach oriented. Let me give you an example: there's a high-tech ministry based out of the Atlanta, Georgia, area that is launching lots of workplace small groups and want non-believing seekers to be involved, and so the small group gatherings are structured accordingly. They are not doing a detailed study of the book of Romans. Rather, they are primarily discussion oriented and topical—Scripture is used, but it's much more of a Bible discussion, not a Bible study. As far as the growth of workplace small groups, focusing on the last two buckets (nominal Christians and non-believers) is where the most growth is happening.

SmallGroups.com: Does the workplace small group have more potential to reach non-believers than the local church?

Steve: No question! It's not even a discussion. Salt and light works better on Monday than Sunday because it wasn't designed to work on Sunday alone. Salt is tasteless when you're designing it for use on Sunday only.

SmallGroups.com: What has been the most effective agenda/format for workplace small groups that are effectively introducing Christ into the workplace?

Steve: I would say most small groups are free flowing rather than being tied to a curriculum. Curriculums that are in use are probably sponsor driven (local church, Promise Keepers, etc.). I don't think there's been one curriculum that has dominated workplace small groups on a national level yet. The more common pattern is to use a format that facilitates a faith-based conversation. We have tried to help folks facilitate a faith-dialogue in the workplace. Let me give you an example. Just this morning I had one of those dialogues. I had been invited to talk with a group of Wal-Mart vendors about the topic of balance in life. Half the managers in attendance had a Bible, half didn't, but we brought biblical principles into the discussion about achieving balance in life and work.

SmallGroups.com: With so much emphasis on team-based approaches to business, are Christians going to be just as effective in changing lives by "living out" Christian community within the existing framework of business teams, or are "lunch-time Bible study groups," still going to be the strategy of choice?

Steve: We have to plan. The water cooler role of influence is legitimate, but we need to be intentional when planning our faith-based influence. The question is, what does that influence look like? Are you implementing Bible-pounding preaching style influence? Or, are you creating safe places that add value to people's lives in authentic ways. People and employers are resistant sometimes to faith-based influences, but if it's adding value to people's lives, and incorporates the upgrade of moral conduct, then employers are generally open. Three things that help make your message persuasive are: is my message meaningful, is my audience receptive, and is my life believable? When your message is appropriate and persuasive, most employers are OK with that. Sure, sometimes in the public work environment, if Christianity is made available then we may have to make other faiths accessible as well, say for instance open the way for a Muslim-led group, but I'm not bothered by that because I've always been a believer that open competition always leans to the one who has the true value.

SmallGroups.com: Without the workplace small group leader having a "pastor" or "overseer" to continually equip and encourage them, how successful have these small groups been at sustaining true Biblical relational community in the workplace?

Steve: To be sustainable, the workplace small group leader needs to develop a support network. This network includes modeling both up, down, and laterally with others who are doing the same thing in order to discover what's working or not working. Sometimes the people who might be included in that network are a church pastor, para-church representative (e.g. Promise Keepers), and other workplace small group leaders in other companies/cities.

SmallGroups.com: Are there ministry organizations that are particularly helpful to Christians who want to influence their workplace for Christ?

Steve: Most workplace ministries are locally-based "mom and pop" organizations. There has not been a great deal of kingdom-wide integration yet. Many are trying to figure out the code of small groups in the workplace. Campus Crusade for Christ's Priority Associates, John Maxwell's Injoy ministries, Os Hillman, and others are leading the way where Life@Work trailed off. Any ministry focused on the workplace needs to be working on the small group community angle of it!

SmallGroups.com: What other insights would you have for Christians in the workplace?

Steve: I've watched the intersection of faith and work for twenty years. The thing I've noticed is that when a Christ-follower's character goes up, many times their skills go down. It's not right that we should follow a God of excellence and not continue to be wrapped up in excellence ourselves, both in character and skills. I would urge workplace small groups to focus on both character and skills when presenting Christ's message. Ultimately that's how we are going to change lives and reach more people for Jesus in our workplace environments. That will create the kind of good clout that we talk about in our book *Clout* from Jossey-Bass.

(This interview originally appeared on SmallGroups.com *in June 2003.)*

Notes

■ Notes

Notes